GOD MET ME HERE:

A Journey to Freedom

BY CHENIER ALSTON

ISBN: 978-1-7369410-4-1

LIBRARY OF CONGRESS CONTROL NUMBER: 2025921316

DEDICATION

I dedicate this book to my beloved wife, Rayna. Thank you for your unwavering love, your strength, and your commitment to helping me see the importance of telling my story. You have always seen the value in me and in this project, even when I struggled to see it myself. Your faith, encouragement, prayers, presence and love made these pages possible. I love you deeply—for who you are, for how you love me, and for reminding me that God's grace is alive in our journey together.

I also dedicate this book to the memory of my late sister, Wenndy J. Prince. Thank you for being one of my greatest supporters, for listening to chapters, and for offering the kind of loving critique that always pushed me to do better. Your encouragement breathed life into this project long before it was complete. I wish you were here to hold this book in your hands, to see the vision fulfilled. I miss you deeply, and I will love you forever.

I also dedicate this book to my beloved parents, Ronnie and Savannah Prince. Thank you for standing with me through every valley and every trial of this journey. I know it was not easy as parents to watch your son walk through the fire, yet what looked like breaking was truly the making of a man called and consecrated by God. Your steadfast love, your unceasing prayers, and your unwavering support carried me when I could not carry myself. Every prayer you lifted was heard, and every tear you shed was not in vain. I felt and experienced your love in the darkest hours, and today, I honor you. This book is as much yours as it is mine.

I also dedicate this book to the memory of Pastor David Lester. Thank you for being a vessel in God's hands during one of the most pivotal seasons of my life. Your words, prayers, and example left an imprint on my spirit that time cannot erase. Though I cannot place this book in your hands, I pray its very existence honors your legacy. May your memory live through these pages until we meet again in the presence of our Lord.

I also dedicate this book to Pastor Colleen Bennette. Thank you for nurturing me in the fragile, formative stages of my faith journey. You believed in what God was birthing in me when I could not yet see it clearly for myself. With love, patience, and unselfish devotion, you poured into my life and calling. For that, I am forever grateful. Thank you, Pastor Bennette—I love you dearly.

And finally, I dedicate this book to my children and grandchildren (Khapri, Kyle, Khari, Julian, Natalia, Natalie, Xoie, KJ, Karter, Kennedy, and Kelani). You are my greatest legacy and my most precious blessing. It is my prayer that when I am long gone, these pages will serve as a reminder that your ultimate source of strength, hope, and salvation is always God. May you never lose sight of His grace, His love, and His power to transform every season of life. I love you all deeply, and I thank you for your unwavering support and encouragement.

TABLE OF CONTENTS

FOREWORD 8

INTRODUCTION 10

CHAPTER ONE A WANTED CHILD............................13

    The Burden Of The Unseen 13

    Revelation..14

    Grace in the Infancy Stage 15

    Satan's Target 15

    Liberated by Grace..16

    Reflection..17

CHAPTER TWO AN IDENTITY CRISIS.........................19

    Unmasking Moses...20

    Unmasking You...22

    Reflection..25

CHAPTER THREE THE BIG BOOM 26

    God in the Shadows 29

    Reflection..32

CHAPTER FOUR A BROKEN DREAM 34

    Broken Dreams...35

    The Power of Illusion 36

    The Fork in the Road 36

    The Deceptive Perspective 37

    Breaking Free from the Illusion....................................37

    Redirection..38

    Reflection..40

CHAPTER FIVE BACK TO THE STREETS 41

Don't Go Back 45

Reflection...48

CHAPTER SIX UNCHARTED TERRITORY **49**

A Pleasant Surprise in an Unexpected Place.................52

Reflection...57

CHAPTER SEVEN WANTED ALIVE BUT DEAD **58**

The Chase 60

Stop Running and Start Facing................................63

Reflection...65

CHAPTER EIGHT THE CALM IN THE STORM...............**67**

Reflection...73

CHAPTER NINE GOD'S PLAN **75**

Reflection...80

CHAPTER TEN NOT GUILTY **81**

The System vs. God's Grace....................................83

Reflection...84

CHAPTER ELEVEN MY JOURNEY TO FREEDOM.........**86**

Reflection...89

CHAPTER TWELVE THE MISSION FIELD **90**

Reflection...93

CHAPTER THIRTEEN DREAMS **95**

The Empowerment Dream 95

The Faith-Inspiring Dream 96

God Still Speaks 97

Five Powerful Ways to Hear God's Voice....................99

Reflection 101

CHAPTER FOURTEEN FAITH ON TRIAL.....................**102**

Day 1 104

Days 2-6 105

Reflection 110

CHAPTER FIFTEEN NOT GUILTY 112

The Verdict of Freedom 114

Living Free, Not Condemned 117

Reflection 118

CHAPTER SIXTEEN DREAMS PART II 120

Reflection 124

CHAPTER SEVENTEEN A SETBACK FOR A COMEBACK
....126

Reflection 131

CHAPTER EIGHTEEN PRISON MINISTRY 132

Reflection 137

CHAPTER NINETEEN LIBERATED BY GRACE 138

MY PRAYER FOR YOU 143

ABOUT THE AUTHOR..144

GOD MET ME HERE

FOREWORD

—=◇◇◇=—

I HAVE HAD THE PRIVILEGE of knowing Pastor Chenier Alston for more than five years, and in that time, I have witnessed a man who embodies integrity, humility, and unwavering faith. His transparency in sharing his personal testimony has not only strengthened me as a believer, but has also sharpened me as a leader in the Kingdom of God.

What you hold in your hands is more than just a book—it is a living testimony of God's power to restore, redeem, and transform. Pastor Alston's journey, from the broken places of his past to the freedom he has found in Christ, speaks to the heart of every person who has ever struggled, stumbled, or felt unworthy of God's grace. From the first chapter to the last, you will be challenged, inspired, and empowered to keep fighting the good fight of faith.

Because God is no respecter of persons, the same supernatural grace that lifted Pastor Alston is available to you. His story will push you to stop running, to start facing the obstacles that hold you back, and to embrace the freedom that only Christ can give.

It is my honor to call Pastor Alston not only a friend, but also a colleague in the work of the Kingdom. I am confident that the message of restoration found in these pages will impact your life as profoundly as it has impacted mine.

PASTOR REGINALD STEELE
KINGDOM CHURCH
PHOENIX, AZ

GOD MET ME HERE

INTRODUCTION

———◇◇◇———

THE CELL WAS COLD. The walls pressed in, heavy with silence that screamed louder than any noise. I remember staring at the ceiling, wondering if this was it... if this was the sum total of my life. The smell of steel and sweat lingered. The sound of clanging doors echoed through the halls. And in the pit of my soul, I felt the weight of every choice I had ever made dragging me down like chains around my neck.

I had tried to be strong. I had tried to numb the pain with the streets, with fast money, with anger, with false power. But in that moment, I had nothing left to hold onto. My identity was stripped. My future seemed sealed. My name, my reputation, my very being felt marked by failure. I was broken... and I believed I was beyond repair.

And then God met me there.

Not in a church pew. Not at an altar. Not in some holy cathedral. He met me in a prison cell. He met me in my shame. He met me in the darkness I thought was permanent. And His presence filled that room with a light I could not explain. It wasn't a physical light, but a light in my spirit, a crack of hope splitting open the night.

I realized something in that moment: God does not wait for us to come to Him polished, perfect, or presentable. He comes to us where we are: broken, battered, and bleeding. And He says, "This is where I'll begin."

That night, I discovered the truth that would change everything: freedom doesn't start when the doors swing open. Freedom starts when grace breaks in. And grace broke into my cell like floodwaters bursting through a dam.

That was the beginning of my journey, the moment God whispered into the silence of my despair and turned my prison into holy ground.

This is my story.

This is my testimony.

This is the journey of how *God Met Me Here: A Journey To Freedom.*

CHAPTER ONE

A WANTED CHILD

SOME MEMORIES CLING TO YOU like shadows, refusing to let go. For me, those shadows often came in the dead of night. As a child, I would wake up trembling, my heart pounding in my chest, my small body drenched in sweat. The nightmare was always the same: an unrelenting, suffocating horror. I was surrounded by frogs, grotesque, otherworldly creatures that exuded malice. These weren't ordinary frogs. Their eyes gleamed with sinister intent, their slimy skin pulsing with an unspoken threat, and their purpose was unmistakable: they wanted to destroy me.

The dream played out like a twisted ritual, over and over again. I would run, desperately searching for safety, but there was no escape. The frogs were relentless, closing in until I could feel their cold, slimy weight pressing against me. Just as their evil intent reached its crescendo, I would wake up, gasping for air, my heart screaming a silent question: Why me?

Even as a child, I sensed there was something deeper behind the terror. I didn't know what, but I knew those dreams weren't just dreams. They clung to me in my waking hours, leaving an invisible mark. Yet I told no one. Who would believe me? How could I possibly explain the fear, the urgency, the weight of it all?

But I knew one thing with absolute certainty: those frogs wanted me dead.

THE BURDEN OF THE UNSEEN

Most children fear imaginary monsters lurking in closets or under beds. My fear was different. It was vivid, tangible, and far too real. These weren't fragments of an overactive imagination. This was something more... a darkness that felt alive, as though it had seeped into my very existence.

I carried the burden in silence, a secret I didn't fully understand. For years, I tried to ignore the recurring nightmare, tried to push it into the recesses of my mind. But it refused to be forgotten. It haunted me, like a dark thread woven into the fabric of my childhood.

It wasn't until years later, when I began to seek God and understand His Word, that I realized the true meaning of those dreams. What I once dismissed as childhood terror was far more profound: I was in the midst of spiritual warfare.

REVELATION

It wasn't until I began to grow in my faith and immerse myself in God's Word that the meaning of those haunting dreams became clear. The answer wasn't merely a product of my imagination but a revelation that shook me to my core, pulled directly from the pages of Scripture:

> *"And I saw three unclean spirits like frogs come out of the mouth of the dragon, out of the mouth of the beast, and out of the mouth of the false prophet."* (Revelation 16:13, NKJV)

The unclean spirits in my dreams were not random figments of fear, they were real. They were demonic forces, agents of deception sent to destroy. Their presence in my childhood nightmares wasn't a coincidence. Even then, before I could grasp the spiritual realm, the enemy had already marked me. He saw something in me I couldn't yet see in myself: a calling, a purpose, a destiny shaped by God's hands.

Satan's plan was insidious and unrelenting. If he could snuff out my potential in its infancy, I would never step into the person God intended me to become. Scripture paints a vivid picture of his strategy:

> *"Your adversary the devil walks about like a roaring lion, seeking whom he may devour"* (1 Peter 5:8)

My recurring dreams were proof of his pursuit. But what he didn't account for, what he couldn't defeat, was the infinite power of God's grace.

GRACE IN THE INFANCY STAGE

Even as a child, vulnerable and unaware, God's grace was already at work in my life. Looking back, I realize that I was a wanted child; not just by Satan, who sought to destroy me, but by God, who claimed me as His own. While the enemy prowled, God's hand shielded me, His grace forming an invisible barrier against the full weight of the attack.

It's a humbling realization to know that God's love and protection were present long before I had the capacity to acknowledge Him. Psalm 139:13-16 paints this truth beautifully: before we are formed in the womb, God knows us. Before we take our first breath, He has written every one of our days in His book. I was cherished, protected, and set apart by God, even in the midst of a battle I didn't know I was fighting.

Those terrifying dreams were proof of His intervention. Each time I woke up, trembling but alive, it was a reminder that the enemy's plans had limits. God didn't allow the darkness to take me. Instead, the dreams became a revelation of the spiritual war over my soul: a war I didn't fight alone.

SATAN'S TARGET

Throughout history, Satan has targeted children. His assaults have always been calculated, aimed at the vulnerable and the innocent, the carriers of tomorrow's purpose. From Pharaoh's decree to kill Hebrew infants in Exodus to Herod's massacre of babies in an attempt to destroy Jesus, the pattern is undeniable. Why does the enemy focus so intently on the young? Because children represent the future. They carry the seeds of transformation, the potential to usher in God's kingdom and dismantle the works of the devil.

I was no different. The enemy recognized the seed of God's purpose within me and sought to destroy it before it could take root. Those frogs in my dream weren't just symbols of fear; they were his early attempts to derail my life. He wanted to crush my destiny before I even understood what it was.

But Satan underestimated the God who authored my story. The battle wasn't his to win.

LIBERATED BY GRACE

God's grace didn't just protect me; it liberated me. As I grew in my faith, I began to recognize the spiritual weapons God provides: prayer, His Word, and the authority of Jesus' name. Each one became a tool to dismantle the enemy's schemes. With them, I discovered the power to rebuke the darkness that once plagued me and to walk boldly in the freedom Christ secured on the cross.

Those dreams, once filled with fear, became a testament to victory. They reminded me of where I had been and how God's grace had carried me through. What the enemy intended for harm, God used for good. And this is just the beginning of the story. What Satan sought to silence, God has amplified. The same grace that shielded me as a child is the grace that empowers me now. It's a grace that is still available to you, to anyone willing to embrace it. The battle is real, but the victory is already won. Will you step into the grace that can transform your life as it did mine?

REFLECTION

1. Have you ever experienced a recurring dream or a significant event that you now recognize as spiritually meaningful? How did it impact your life or perspective?

2. How do you interpret the idea that the enemy might see your potential before you do? In what ways might this influence how you view challenges in your life?

3. When you read about the unclean spirits described in Revelation, what thoughts or emotions come to mind? How do you see spiritual warfare playing a role in your own life?

4. Reflect on a time in your life when you felt protected or guided, even if you didn't recognize it at the time. What does this reveal about God's presence in your life?

5. Psalm 139 speaks of being known by God before birth. How does this knowledge affect how you view your purpose and worth?

6. The chapter mentions being "wanted by God." How does this idea resonate with you personally?

7. Why do you think Satan focuses so intently on targeting children or those in vulnerable stages of life? Have you seen this pattern in your own experiences or in the world around you?

8. The chapter highlights the importance of understanding your role in God's kingdom. How might this awareness change how you respond to challenges or attacks on your purpose?

9. How do you feel about the idea that your life carries a God-ordained destiny that threatens the kingdom of darkness?

10. What spiritual weapons (prayer, Scripture, or the name of Jesus) do you currently rely on during times of

spiritual attack? Are there any you feel called to strengthen?

11. How has God's grace liberated you from a struggle, fear, or destructive path in your life?

12. After reading this chapter, what steps can you take to deepen your understanding of and reliance on God's grace in your daily life?

CHAPTER TWO

AN IDENTITY CRISIS

ONE OF THE GREATEST RESPONSIBILITIES of parenting is shaping a child's identity. When a child is left to define themselves, the results can be devastating. Proverbs 22:6 admonishes us, "Train up a child in the way he should go, and when he is old he will not depart from it." This is not merely about teaching right from wrong but about providing the foundation upon which a child builds their sense of self. A child left to wander in the wilderness of identity without guidance is vulnerable to the winds of circumstance, the opinions of others, and the lies they begin to tell themselves.

As I look back, I realize that no one defined who I was. I grew up suffering from an identity crisis, and I didn't even know it at the time. No one told me I could become a doctor, a lawyer, a business owner, or even the pastor I am today. My surroundings and circumstances stepped in where people failed. They became the loudest voices in shaping my self-perception.

I grew up in an environment where resources were scarce. We didn't have the newest or nicest clothes. Our shoes were worn, and the fabric of our shirts and pants bore the visible scars of wear and tear. The kids at school didn't let us forget it. They mocked us for the very things we couldn't control: the clothes we wore, the brands and labels we could not afford. Every day at school felt like stepping into a battlefield where my self-esteem was under siege.

What I didn't know then was that the laughter of those kids, the finger-pointing, and the ridicule were chiseling away at the tender parts of me. I became the kid who was ashamed of what I wore.

In the absence of someone to guide me toward a true sense of identity, I created a version of myself that I thought could survive the cruelty of the world. I became a fighter.

Fighting became my armor. It became my voice in a world that often silenced me. It was how I demanded respect when I couldn't earn it through academic success, financial stability, or social standing.

But behind every punch thrown, there was a deeper reality. I wasn't fighting just to stand up to the bullies. I was fighting to protect the kid I was hiding. I used this tough exterior to shield the vulnerable boy inside: the boy who was made fun of, who didn't know who he was, and who desperately wanted to belong.

Yet, this self-created image of strength brought its own complications. While I projected toughness to the world, I carried an internal conflict that tore at me daily. Who was I really? Was I the fighter who refused to back down, or was I the scared, vulnerable child trying to escape ridicule and demand respect? The truth was, I didn't know. I was lost, floundering in the vast space between who I was and who I pretended to be.

As I grew older, the identity crisis didn't simply vanish; it evolved. The teenage years brought new challenges, and the stakes felt higher. I learned that the world didn't judge you by what you wore but by what you achieved, who you associated with, and how you presented yourself. I struggled to meet the standards set by society because I didn't have the tools or the confidence to believe I could succeed.

UNMASKING MOSES

Moses is a profound biblical example of an identity crisis. From the moment his mother placed him in a basket and sent him down the Nile River (Exodus 2:2), external circumstances shaped Moses' identity. Rescued by Pharaoh's daughter, he was given an Egyptian name and raised as royalty (Exodus 2:5-10). Yet, at his core, Moses was Hebrew, born into a people oppressed and enslaved. This duality of identity created deep internal conflict, as he lived outwardly like an Egyptian but inwardly carried the burden of his Hebrew heritage.

Moses' unresolved identity crisis led to a breaking point when he witnessed an Egyptian beating a Hebrew slave.

Overwhelmed by the tension between who he was and who he was pretending to be, Moses committed premeditated murder (Exodus 2:11-12). His inability to reconcile his true self with his external identity resulted in his fleeing to Midian, where he spent years grappling with his purpose.

This story illustrates a timeless truth: when we allow others or circumstances to define who we are, it can lead to chaos and self-destruction. Identity must be grounded in truth, not external labels or expectations. Only when Moses embraced his God-given identity did he step into his purpose as Israel's deliverer.

Just like Moses, I wrestled with an identity that didn't fit the calling in my heart. Moses was raised in Pharaoh's palace, surrounded by the trappings of Egyptian royalty, yet deep within, he was an Israelite, connected to a suffering people and a greater purpose. That dissonance drove him to moments of confusion and despair, much like it did for me.

The identity I created for myself, crafted from my environment, circumstances, and survival instincts, was a mask. It gave me power, protection, and respect in the streets. But it also imprisoned me. On the outside, I was a gangbanger, projecting toughness and dominance. But on the inside, a peaceful person longed to lay down the weapons, step out of the chaos, and find rest. I silenced that part of me, dismissing it as weakness in a world where vulnerability was dangerous.

As a drug dealer, I wore the mask of control and authority, creating an image of someone who had life figured out, someone untouchable. Yet, beneath that facade was a man full of hope and optimism, yearning for something greater, something honest and meaningful. The hopeful part of me often whispered dreams of a different life: one where I could use my gifts to uplift, not destroy. But those whispers were drowned out by the roar of survival.

And then there was the fighter. Fighting wasn't just something I did; it became who I was. My fists spoke when my heart couldn't, and I wore my anger like armor. But underneath the fighter was a loving man, someone who craved connection and belonging. The loving man wanted to embrace life and people, but the fighter told him love was weakness, and that to survive, I had to be hard, cold, and unrelenting.

This constant silencing of my inner self was exhausting. Each time I ignored the whispers of my soul, I felt a deeper sadness, a nagging sense of unfulfillment that no amount of money, respect, or power could erase. It was only later that I realized this inner conflict was not a sign of failure but an invitation: a call to let grace reconcile my divided self and lead me to a truer, freer identity.

UNMASKING YOU

In a world that often feels chaotic and unpredictable, it can be easy to let the storms we face shape how we see ourselves. Broken relationships, career setbacks, financial struggles, or even the pain of past mistakes can create an identity rooted in chaos. We begin to define ourselves by our wounds rather than our worth, by our scars rather than our Savior. But I'm here to remind you that who you are is not dictated by the chaos you've been through. Your true identity is rooted in who God has created you to be, someone who is fearfully and wonderfully made.

The enemy delights in using chaos to distort your sense of self. When life becomes overwhelming, he whispers lies that convince you that you are unworthy, unloved, or irreparably broken. He tries to brand you with the identity of failure, victim, or outcast. But these labels are not from God. They are the product of a world that seeks to separate you from the truth of who you are in Christ.

Psalm 139:14 declares, "I praise you because I am fearfully and wonderfully made; your works are wonderful, I know that full well." These words are not just poetic encouragement; they are a divine declaration about your worth and purpose. God took meticulous care in creating you, crafting every detail with intention and love. He did not make a mistake when He formed you, and He has not abandoned you in your struggles. The chaos of life may try to tell you otherwise, but God's truth is unchanging: you are His masterpiece.

It's important to recognize that identity crises often stem from misplaced focus. When we allow our circumstances to define us, we lose sight of who God says we are. For example, if you've experienced rejection, you might begin to believe that you are unlovable. If you've failed in a significant way, you might start to see yourself as a failure. But these identities are false. They are distortions that arise when we look to the world's chaos for answers instead of looking to God's Word.

In John 10:10, Jesus reminds us of His purpose:

"The thief comes only to steal and kill and destroy; I have come that they may have life, and have it to the full."

The thief, the enemy of your soul, wants to steal your identity and destroy your confidence in who God made you to be. But Jesus came to give you a full and abundant life: a life where your identity is secure in Him. He calls you beloved, redeemed, and chosen. He sees beyond your chaos to the person He designed you to be.

So how do you reclaim your God-given identity in the midst of chaos? It begins with surrender. Lay down the false identities you've been clinging to and invite God to redefine who you are. Spend time in His Word, where He reveals the truth about your worth and purpose. Surround yourself with people who will remind you of your true identity and speak life into your spirit. Pray for the strength to silence the lies of the enemy and embrace the truth of God's promises.

It's also important to remember that your identity in Christ is not contingent on perfection. You don't have to have it all together to be loved by God. Romans 5:8 tells us, "But God demonstrates his own love for us in this: While we were still sinners, Christ died for us." His love for you is not based on your performance or your ability to navigate life's chaos. It is based on His unchanging nature and His infinite grace.

As you journey through life, challenges will come, and chaos will attempt to shake your foundation. But stand firm in the truth that your identity is not up for debate. You are not the sum of your mistakes, nor are you defined by your struggles. You are a child of God, created in His image and called for His purpose. Embrace the identity He has given you and walk boldly in the freedom of His grace. Remember, you are fearfully and wonderfully made, and nothing, not even chaos, can change that.

REFLECTION

1. What false identities or labels have you believed about yourself, and how have they shaped your decisions?

2. How does knowing that you are fearfully and wonderfully made change your perspective on your worth?

3. What steps can you take to replace lies from the enemy with the truth found in God's Word?

4. Are there specific Bible verses or promises that remind you of your true identity? How can you meditate on these daily?

5. Who in your life speaks truth into your identity, and how can you strengthen those relationships?

6. How have past challenges or failures influenced your self-image, and what truths counter those narratives?

7. What does it mean to surrender your identity to God, and what areas of your life need His redefinition?

8. How can prayer help you silence the negative voices in your mind and reinforce God's truth?

9. What practical actions can you take to guard against allowing chaos to define you?

10. How does understanding God's unconditional love impact the way you see yourself during difficult times?

11. What opportunities do you have to encourage others to embrace their God-given identity?

12. How can gratitude for God's design and purpose for your life strengthen your sense of identity?

CHAPTER THREE

THE BIG BOOM

WHEN I GRADUATED from high school, I was standing at the edge of a vast, empty field of possibilities. But instead of feeling liberated by the openness, I felt lost. I had no clear direction, no purpose, and no plan for my future. Many of my peers were heading to college, trade schools, or straight into the workforce. For me, though, none of those paths felt right, or maybe I was just too scared to commit to one. Instead, I drifted into a world that had already started pulling at me: the drug game.

It wasn't a sudden decision. Looking back, it was like stepping into quicksand: one choice after another pulling me deeper. I found myself spending more and more time with a group of older guys who were already knee-deep in the game. They had everything I thought I wanted: fancy cars with rims that gleamed in the sunlight, closets full of designer clothes, pockets overflowing with cash, and a type of power and respect that seemed magnetic. Wherever they went, people noticed, and that kind of attention was intoxicating for a young man searching for his identity.

But there was another side to me, a quieter voice inside that wrestled with these temptations. I wanted more out of life than flashy material things. I didn't want to be just another statistic. Deep down, I longed for meaning and purpose, but at that moment, I didn't know how to find it. The pull of the lifestyle was strong, and I was too inexperienced to see the trap being set for me.

The real tipping point came when my older brother moved into an apartment complex in Harvey called the Nine, located on 159th and Lexington. He didn't sugarcoat what he told me about the place: "Man, it's booming over here." In the drug world, "booming" wasn't just a word; it was a siren call. It meant the money was flowing, the business was thriving, and everyone involved was eating well.

26

At first, his words were just a curiosity to me, a spark in the back of my mind. But as days went by, that spark grew into a flame. I couldn't stop wondering what it was like. Was it really as crazy as he described? Finally, my former best friend and I decided to take a trip over there to see for ourselves.

What we found was exactly what my brother had described, and more. It was chaos, but not the kind you ran from, it was organized chaos, like Black Friday at Walmart. People lined up in droves, cash in hand, ready to buy whatever was on offer. Cars pulled in and out of the lot like a never-ending carousel. The air buzzed with energy, the kind that makes your heart race. Everyone seemed to have a role, a purpose. And then there was the money. It wasn't just being made; it was being flaunted. Wads of cash exchanged hands like it was Monopoly money.

I wanted in. The temptation was too much to resist. I saw an opportunity to get what I thought I needed—money, respect, and a sense of belonging. My brother saw the hunger in my eyes and decided to introduce me to the man in charge of the Nine, a man everyone called Big Boom. He wasn't just a nickname; he was the embodiment of everything the Nine represented. People spoke his name with both reverence and fear. He was the head of the operation, the man pulling the strings.

When I met Big Boom, he wasn't what I expected. He wasn't loud or flashy. He had a calm, almost calculated demeanor, the kind that made you instantly respect him. My brother vouched for me, and that gave me a foot in the door. But getting in wasn't just about knowing someone; I had to prove myself.

That chance came almost immediately. A man owed him money, and it was clear from the look on his face that he wasn't planning to pay up. Big Boom wasn't the kind of man who tolerated disrespect, and he made it clear he wanted the situation handled.

Without thinking too much about it, I stepped up. "I can take care of it," I told him. He looked at me for a moment, sizing me up. Then, with a slight nod, he gave me the green light.

What happened next was like flipping a switch inside me. I approached the man and, without hesitation, unleashed a barrage of punches. The adrenaline coursing through me drowned out everything else. The sounds around me blurred, and all I could feel was the raw surge of energy. By the time I stopped, the man was down, and I was left breathing hard, my fists aching.

That was it. That was my initiation, even though I felt the guilt of my actions. Big Boom saw something in me that day: loyalty, fearlessness, or maybe just a willingness to do what others wouldn't. Whatever it was, he decided I was worth taking under his wing. From that moment on, I was one of his guys, part of the set at the Nine.

Looking back, I can see how pivotal that moment was. It wasn't just about joining the set or making money. It was the beginning of a journey that would take me to places I never expected to go, which were bad. I thought I was stepping into a world of power and opportunity, but what I didn't realize was that I was also stepping into a world of darkness, danger, and soul-crushing consequences.

At the time, though, I didn't see any of that. All I saw was the allure of the lifestyle, the promises it seemed to hold. I didn't know that every choice I made from that point on would come with a price. All I knew was that I was in, and there was no turning back.

That was the big boom for me, the explosion that set my life on a trajectory I couldn't fully comprehend. It would take years, pain, and ultimately grace to break free from the chains I willingly put on that day. But for now, I was flying high, caught up in the thrill of it all, oblivious to the storm clouds gathering on the horizon.

GOD IN THE SHADOWS

I previously stated I had started hanging out with some older guys who were deep in the drug game. They had the flash: the cars, the cash, and the kind of respect that turned heads wherever they went. For me, searching for identity and validation, that life seemed alluring, almost magnetic. I wanted to be part of their world, to stand where they stood and feel the power they seemed to wield. But no matter how close I got to them, there was a line they wouldn't let me cross.

They allowed me into their circle, just enough to feel like I belonged but never enough to fully engage in what they were doing. They let me drive their cars, ride shotgun to places I had no business being, and soak up the attention their status afforded. But they didn't let me sell drugs. I wondered why. Was it a test of my loyalty? Were they trying to figure out if I was trustworthy or if I could handle the weight of their world? Or maybe they only kept me around because I brought something to the table, like connections to my female friends, some of whom were undeniably beautiful.

I didn't have answers then, and honestly, I didn't spend much time trying to find them. I was too caught up in the excitement of being close to something I thought I wanted. What I did know, however, was that I wasn't allowed to get involved in the actual business of drugs. At the time, I saw it as a frustration, a barrier keeping me from fully embracing what I thought was the path to success. But later in life, after God changed my heart and opened my eyes, I realized that this was no coincidence. It was God, quietly working in the background, shielding me from a world that would have consumed me whole.

Once I eventually joined the set at the Nine, I got a taste of what that life was really like. The glamour I had once admired was quickly overshadowed by chaos. Life became fast-paced, and while the money came quickly, so did the problems. The nights were filled with violence and unpredictability. Every dollar seemed to come with a cost, and that cost was often paid in blood, fear, or regret. The things I once thought were marks of success: the cars, the cash, and the respect were nothing more than illusions, masking the pain and danger lurking beneath the surface.

It was only after I left that life behind and surrendered to God that I began to see how God had been operating all along. In high school, I thought the older guys were protecting their turf or keeping me on the sidelines for their own reasons. But now I see that God was using them, perhaps unknowingly, as instruments of His will to keep me from diving headfirst into the drug game at a young age. By not allowing me to get fully involved with them, He spared me from becoming entangled in the kind of violence that claimed so many lives. Some of those men I once admired didn't make it out. They fell victim to the very lifestyle I once thought was the pinnacle of success.

When I was part of the Nine, God continued to work, even when I couldn't see it. There were countless nights when things could have gone horribly wrong. Times when bullets flew past me, when tempers flared, and when the weight of the choices I was making could have crushed me. Yet, somehow, I was preserved. I didn't see it then, but I can see it now. Every close call, every moment where I narrowly avoided disaster, was a testament to God's hand over my life.

It's humbling to look back and realize that even in my rebellion, even when I was chasing after things that had no lasting value, God was there. He was guiding me, protecting me, and keeping me from fully self-destructing. His grace didn't just show up when I decided to turn my life around. It was there all along, working in ways I couldn't understand or appreciate at the time.

I think about the friends I lost along the way, the ones who didn't make it out. Some were gunned down in senseless acts of violence; others were swallowed up by addiction or locked away behind bars. Their stories could have been my story. By all rights, I should have been another statistic, another young man consumed by the streets. But God had other plans for me.

His grace was my shield, even when I didn't recognize it. It was the quiet force that kept me from stepping too far into a world that would have destroyed me. And now, as I reflect on those years, I am filled with gratitude. Gratitude for a God who doesn't give up on us, even when we're running in the opposite direction. Gratitude for His grace that operates in the shadows, protecting us from dangers we can't even see. I couldn't see it then, but now I know: His grace was always there, working on my behalf, setting the stage for the redemption that was yet to come.

The Apostle Paul reminds us in 2 Corinthians 12:9 that God's grace is sufficient for us, and His power is made perfect in weakness. This scripture is a profound reminder that grace doesn't depend on our circumstances. It's not restricted to moments when life is going well or when we feel strong. Instead, grace thrives in the shadows, in the midst of pain, fear, and uncertainty.

When you reflect on your life, can you recall moments when you thought you wouldn't make it through, but somehow, you did? Perhaps it was a time of loss, betrayal, or failure, and though you felt abandoned, you found the strength to carry on. That's grace. It may not have looked like a "big boom," but it was real and transformative. God's grace works behind the curtain of our lives, stitching together the fragments of our brokenness into something beautiful.

REFLECTION

1. Can you recall a time when things felt hopeless, but something unexpected happened that gave you strength or clarity? How might that have been a sign of grace?

2. Have you ever experienced a moment where you felt undeserving of help or forgiveness, yet it was given to you? How did it impact your perspective?

3. What small, seemingly ordinary moments in your day might actually be examples of God's grace at work?

4. Are there areas in your life where you've experienced healing or growth, even if the process was slow or painful? How might God have been shaping you during that time?

5. How has God's grace shown itself through the people in your life, perhaps through their kindness, support, or encouragement?

6. Have you ever been forgiven by someone when you didn't expect it? How does that reflect God's grace in action?

7. Can you identify a moment when you felt God's presence or provision during a particularly dark or challenging season?

8. When something you hoped for didn't work out, can you now see how grace may have been protecting or redirecting you?

9. What are three things you are grateful for today that might reveal God's grace operating behind the scenes?

10. How often do you intentionally reflect on the small ways God provides for you daily? What could help you become more aware of these moments?

11. What areas of your life do you feel need the most grace right now? How can trusting God's unseen work bring you peace?

12. How might reflecting on past experiences of grace in the shadows encourage you to trust God more fully in the uncertainties of life?

CHAPTER FOUR
A BROKEN DREAM

AFTER HIGH SCHOOL, I was fully immersed in the drug world on 159th Street, better known as the Nine. Everything moved at a relentless pace. There was no time to slow down, no room to hesitate. The money came in fast, and with it came the rush, the power, the respect. My street cred as a hustler was growing, solidifying my place in the game. Every transaction, every nod of acknowledgment from those who ran the streets, added to the weight of my name. But that life was unpredictable, always on edge, with the constant hum of danger in the air. One wrong move could change everything, yet that uncertainty was part of the thrill.

Still, while I was neck-deep in the life, I found myself trapped in what I call a terrible pull and an awful push. The pull came from something deep inside me, a quiet but persistent voice telling me I was meant for more. It was the urge to rise above my surroundings, to make something of myself beyond the Nine. But at the same time, there was a force pushing me toward the streets, the environment, the loyalty, the easy money, the reputation. The streets had a way of pulling you in, making it feel like there was no other option, like the Nine was both the beginning and the end of everything.

For a while, the terrible pull seemed to be winning. Before I got caught up in the drug game, before my name carried weight on the Nine, I had already made a decision most people around me wouldn't have expected: I signed up for the military. It was a choice that felt like an escape, a way to rewrite my story before it was written for me. But I didn't tell many people. The only ones who knew were my parents, my oldest brother, cousins who also were out there hustling with me, and my girlfriend at the time. They were the only ones who understood, the only ones I trusted with that part of me.

The plan was set in motion, and I was set to leave in October of 1990. I was stationed in Fort Leonard Wood, Missouri. It was bitterly cold there. Basic training was difficult. I experienced homesickness. My mind constantly wandered back to the Nine. I wondered what my brother and cousins were doing. Were they making money? Were they being careful? I worried about them, but I kept reminding myself: this was my chance to be all I could be. That was Uncle Sam's selling point, right? "Be all that you can be."

But my dreams came to an abrupt halt one day while running during training. A sharp, unfamiliar pain shot through my knee, sending me crashing to the ground. I couldn't continue the drills. I was put on crutches while the Army doctors decided what to do. Eventually, they determined my injury must have existed before I enlisted. They deemed it not worth the time or resources to operate, rehab, and retrain me because the Gulf War was moving into action; they needed soldiers to go to war. So, just like that, they issued me a general discharge.

On December 16, 1990, I packed my bags, collected my final check, and was sent home. My shot at becoming someone great the right way had been taken from me. And the only thing waiting for me back home was the Nine.

BROKEN DREAMS

Dreams are the fuel that ignites our ambitions, the visions that keep us pressing forward even in the face of adversity. However, when dreams shatter, they leave behind fragments of doubt, fear, and despair. A broken dream can feel like the end of everything: a definitive stop sign on the road of life. Yet, the reality is that broken dreams are often illusionary; they present a false narrative that convinces us all is lost when, in truth, it is not. They blind us to the possibilities that remain, distorting our vision so that we only see destruction and ruin where new opportunities may still exist.

I know this firsthand. When I learned I was being generally discharged from the Army, it felt like my entire world was collapsing. Everything I had worked for, everything I envisioned for my future, seemed to vanish in an instant. The pain of that moment was more than disappointment; it was devastation. In my mind, I was left with only one option: to return to the Nine and sell drugs. My broken dream had convinced me that there was no other road, no other direction I could take. But that was an illusion. A broken dream can lead you down a dark path, but it does not mean that path is the only one available. It just means that, for a time, you have been deceived into believing so.

THE POWER OF ILLUSION

When a dream breaks, it does more than just disappoint; it reshapes your entire perception of reality. It convinces you that the world is now limited, that choices have been stripped away, and that failure is your only inheritance. Broken dreams have a way of narrowing your vision, erasing the possibility of alternatives. They whisper in your ear that you have nothing left, that you are stuck in a singular fate. This is what happened to me when I lost my military career. The illusion told me I was unworthy, unfit for anything better, and incapable of climbing out of the hole I found myself in.

But an illusion, by definition, is not real. It is a false image, a mirage that deceives the mind into believing in something that does not truly exist. A broken dream is a lie because it suggests that you have no future when in reality, you do. It tells you there is only one way forward: the road to ruin. But that is simply not true.

THE FORK IN THE ROAD

One of the most dangerous aspects of broken dreams is their ability to erase our sense of direction. They convince us that there is no fork in the road, only a single path leading to perdition. This is what happened to me. When I lost my footing in the Army, I did not see a fork in the road; I saw the Nine. I believed that my past was my only option and that returning to the streets was inevitable. But that was not reality. The fork in the road existed all along; I just had to open my eyes to see it.

In every moment of despair, there is always a choice. The problem is that broken dreams obscure our peripheral vision, making us believe that we have no options when, in truth, we always do. Just because one door has closed does not mean another is not waiting to be opened. Looking back on it now I realized that my past did not have to define my future. The streets were not my destiny. I had the power to choose a different path, one that led to growth rather than destruction.

THE DECEPTIVE PERSPECTIVE

A broken dream gives you tunnel vision that distorts reality. Instead of seeing the full picture, you become fixated on what was lost. Your mind replays the failure over and over again, drowning out any thoughts of hope or possibility. This is the great deception of shattered dreams: they make you believe that your story is over when, in fact, it is still being written.

I allowed that broken dream of being all I can be through the military to dictate my actions. I let it shape my perspective, convincing me that I had no worth outside of the life I planned for. But what I failed to realize was that the only thing truly holding me back was my own belief in the illusion. Had I broken free from that mindset, I would have seen at that moment there were paths I had never considered. I saw that I was more than my failures, more than my mistakes. I had the ability to rebuild, to reinvent myself, and to move forward in ways I had never imagined.

BREAKING FREE FROM THE ILLUSION

So how does one break free from the illusion of broken dreams? How does one learn to see the fork in the road when all they see is a dead end? It begins with a shift in perspective. Instead of focusing on what was lost, focus on what remains. Instead of mourning the dream that has shattered, consider the new dreams that can be built from the pieces.

1. ALLOW GOD TO REDESIGN YOU AND YOUR FUTURE.

2. ACKNOWLEDGE THE PAIN, BUT DO NOT DWELL IN IT: It is natural to grieve a lost dream, but staying trapped in that grief will only prolong the illusion. Acknowledge your pain, but do not let it define you.

3. SEEK GUIDANCE AND SUPPORT: We are not meant to navigate life's struggles alone. Seek wisdom from those who have walked similar paths. Surround yourself with people who see beyond your current circumstances and can help you envision a brighter future.

4. REEVALUATE YOUR STRENGTHS AND PURPOSE: Just because one avenue has closed does not mean your purpose has disappeared. Consider your skills, talents, and passions. There are other ways to use them.

5. TAKE SMALL STEPS FORWARD: The road to redemption is not walked in a single stride. It takes time, patience, and perseverance. Every small step away from the illusion is a step toward the truth.

6. STRENGTHEN YOUR FAITH: In times of despair, faith is the anchor that keeps us from drifting into hopelessness. Trust that God has a plan even when you cannot see it. Trust that He is working all things together for your good.

REDIRECTION

Looking back, I realize that my broken dream was not the end of my story. It was simply a turning point, a moment that forced me to make a choice: stay trapped in the illusion or break free and move forward. At the time I chose the trappings of the illusion. I chose to believe that my life was only relegated to the Nine, not realizing that I had more to offer, and that there was still purpose ahead of me.

If you are struggling with a broken dream, know that you are not alone. Know that what feels like the end is often just the beginning of something new. The illusion will try to convince you that all is lost but do not believe it. God always places a fork in the road. There is always another way. You just have to be willing to see it.

Broken dreams may shake us, but they do not have to break us. The illusion may be powerful, but the truth is stronger. The truth is that you are not defined by a single failure or failing event. You are not condemned to a single path. You have choices. You have a future. You have a purpose.

And that purpose is still waiting for you to step into it.

REFLECTION

1. How have broken dreams influenced your perception of yourself and your future?

2. Can you recall a time when a broken dream made you feel like all was lost? How did you respond?

3. What illusions have your past failures created in your mind?

4. In what ways have you struggled to see the "fork in the road" when facing disappointment?

5. How do you think faith and perseverance can help in overcoming the illusion of broken dreams?

6. What small steps can you take today to move beyond a past failure?

7. Who in your life can serve as a source of guidance and encouragement when facing setbacks?

8. What talents, strengths, or passions do you still have that could lead you toward a new purpose?

9. How does focusing on what remains, rather than what is lost, shift your mindset?

10. Have you ever realized later that what seemed like a failure was actually leading you to something better?

11. What role does self-forgiveness play in overcoming the deception of broken dreams?

12. How can you encourage others who may be struggling with the illusion that their dreams are permanently shattered?

CHAPTER FIVE

BACK TO THE STREETS

MY DREAM OF BECOMING SOMEONE through a military career was now in the rearview mirror of my life. The vision I had for my future of being all I can be was over. As I walked through the airport terminal, a heavy weight settled on my shoulders. My mother was waiting for me just outside baggage claim, and when I saw her, I could tell she was trying to gauge how I was feeling. She greeted me with a warm hug, but I barely felt it. My mind was elsewhere.

The ride home was quiet. My mother occasionally glanced at me, but she didn't say much. Maybe she knew I wasn't ready to talk, or maybe she was afraid of what I might say. Either way, I stared out of the window, watching the familiar city streets blur past. My thoughts weren't on home, at least not the home she had prepared for me. No, my thoughts were on the Nine.

As soon as I put my bags up, I made my way over there. My mother didn't even have to ask where I was going; she knew. I could feel her eyes on my back as I stepped out the door, but she didn't try to stop me. Maybe she knew she couldn't.

The Nine hadn't changed. The moment I arrived, it was as if I had stepped right back into the world I had left behind. The set was busy as usual. Cars were lined up, headlights illuminating the figures of workers sprinting to and from the vehicles, money exchanging hands as quickly as the drugs that fueled the business. The night air was biting, a freezing wind cutting through the block, but the hustle never stopped. Neither did the addiction.

As I stepped out of the car, the cold air hit me, but it wasn't long before warmth surrounded me. My people greeted me with open arms. The gang was shocked to see me; their faces lit up with recognition and excitement.

41

"Aye, look who it is!" one of them shouted. "The soldier boy home!"

Laughter erupted, followed by jokes about my clean-shaven face. They teased me about the military's strict grooming standards, but beneath the jokes was genuine love. I could feel it. I had been gone, but I was still one of them. That was what I needed to feel at that moment: belonging.

But something was missing.

I scanned the set, looking for my brothers and cousins. They weren't out there. That struck me as odd. The Nine had always been their domain. When I asked where they were, one of the guys nodded toward one of the apartment buildings.

"They inside, bro. They been low for a minute."

That answer didn't sit right with me. I made my way to the apartment, knocked on the door, and waited. When my cousin opened it and saw me standing there, he didn't say a word. He just grabbed me, pulling me into a tight embrace. One by one, my family followed suit, and for a moment, all was right. For a moment, I wasn't a man trying to figure out what came next; I was just home.

But the moment didn't last.

Once the initial excitement of my return settled, the reality of their situation became clear. My brothers had fallen off. In the world we lived in, that was a heavy thing. It wasn't just about money; it was about survival. A drought had hit the city hard, and they hadn't been able to keep up. The streets were merciless. If you weren't making money, you weren't just broke; you were vulnerable. You were a liability. I saw the stress in their faces and the frustration in their eyes. I didn't have to ask how bad it was. I could see it.

Without a word, I reached into my pocket, pulled out my military check, and placed it on the table. "Let's use this so that we can get back in the game," I said.

Silence filled the room. My brothers looked at me, then at the check, then back at me. They were processing what I had just done, what I had just said.

At that moment, it felt like the most natural decision in the world. What else was I supposed to do? The military was gone. The future I had envisioned had been stripped away. But the streets? The streets were still here. They had never left me, and now, I was choosing not to leave them.

I told myself I was doing it for my family. That I couldn't stand to see them struggling. That I was stepping in to help, to bring stability back to what we had built. But deep down, I knew the truth. I wasn't just doing it for them. I was doing it because I didn't know who I was without the structure the military had given me. I was doing it because, without the uniform, I felt lost. And when you're lost, you go back to what's familiar. You go back to what you know.

The illusion of broken dreams had convinced me that I had no other choice. That the Nine was my only option. And in that moment, I believed it.

The game was back on. I was back on the streets!

We took the money I received from the military and flipped it, turning it into something that would either save us or destroy us. The drugs sold fast, too fast. The money poured in like a flood, drowning out any doubts I had left. We weren't just back on our feet; we were running at full speed, back in the game as if we had never left. But with every dollar stacked, the weight of what we were doing grew heavier. The streets only know how to curse you.

With success came problems; problems I had seen before but never fully understood until I was in the thick of them. Friends started eyeing us differently. Smiles became forced, and handshakes became tense. The same people who once befriended us now whispered in the shadows, their jealousy turning to resentment. I could feel the shift in the air, the unspoken tension tightening around us like a noose. Violence wasn't just a possibility; it was inevitable. I could sense it lurking around every corner, waiting for the right moment to strike.

Sleep became a luxury I couldn't afford. My body ached for rest, but my mind wouldn't let me have it. Every night, I lay awake with my gun by my side, my ears tuned to every sound outside my window. A car rolling by too slowly, footsteps lingering where they shouldn't: everything felt like a threat. I was constantly looking over my back, waiting for the moment when it would all come crashing down.

And then the streets turned on us. The very people we had grown up with, the ones who had once called us brothers, now saw us as enemies. The Nine, our home, had become a war zone, and we were the targets. I couldn't understand it: how quickly love could turn into hate, how greed could turn blood against blood. Every move we made had to be calculated; every conversation was analyzed for hidden motives. Trust? That was a joke. Trust could get you killed.

And as if that wasn't enough, the law was never far behind. Every day, I lived with the gnawing fear of flashing red and blue lights, of being thrown against a squad car, of hearing the metal clink of handcuffs locking around my wrists. Prison wasn't just a possibility; it was a shadow that followed me everywhere. The paranoia was unbearable, suffocating. I could feel it pressing down on my chest, making it hard to breathe. I wasn't free. I was caged, trapped in a life I had walked back into with my eyes wide open but my soul blind to the cost.

This was my reality. This was what I had returned to. And there appeared to be no silver lining to it.

I didn't want this life. I wanted peace. I wanted freedom. I wanted something that didn't come with the weight of death and betrayal hanging over my head. The money was good, more money than I had ever seen at one time, but what good was it if every dollar felt like another chain dragging me down? The cost of it all: my sanity, my safety, my soul was growing heavier with every passing day.

I had convinced myself I had no other option, that this was the only road left for me. But now, standing in the center of it all, surrounded by enemies disguised as friends and money that felt more like a curse than a blessing, I realized something chilling.

The streets had welcomed me back, but they weren't going to let me go so easily.

DON'T GO BACK

There are moments in life where we stand at a crossroads, where our next decision will shape everything that comes after it. I remember that moment vividly. I had a choice: to take the money I had left from the military and invest it in my future, or to return to the only thing I thought I knew: the streets. I should have chosen differently. I should have taken that money and gone to school, learned a trade, built something that could last. But I didn't. I went back. And if there's one thing I can tell you, it's this: going back to something nonbeneficial, something destructive, something that once had its grip on you, it's never worth it.

Maybe you're reading this right now, and you're at your crossroads. Maybe you're thinking about going back to a life that God already gave you the grace to walk away from. Perhaps it's the streets, maybe it's an unhealthy relationship, an addiction, a cycle of self-destruction that once consumed you. Whatever it is, let me be real with you: it doesn't get better. The streets don't get better. The habits that once nearly destroyed you don't suddenly become safe. The toxic environment that God freed you from won't magically change just because time has passed. The past is just that: your past. It was never meant for you to live in.

Looking back, I see it so clearly. The streets weren't built for success. They weren't made for growth. They were designed to pull you in, keep you locked in place, and, if you let them, bury you. When I went back, I thought I was just picking up where I had left off. I thought I could handle it, that somehow I had outgrown the dangers. But I was wrong. The moment I stepped back in, it was as if no time had passed. The same dangers, the same enemies disguised as friends, the same sleepless nights, the same paranoia: it was all still there, waiting for me. And it's waiting for you, too, if you choose to go back.

I know how it feels to be stuck between what you know and what you can't yet see. It is a very contentious place to be in because it makes you think that your future seems uncertain and unfamiliar. It tries to convince you that going back to the broken thing you once depended on is what's best. It makes you believe that the streets' promise of fast money is sustaining. That fake relationships are the key to comfort. And that addiction whispers relief. But it's all a lie. It's an illusion meant to keep you from the purpose God has for you. The enemy will always try to convince you that you have no other options, that this is all you know, and that you don't have the resources or the ability to start over. But let me tell you something: God always has another way. Always.

Every day you wake up, every breath you take is another opportunity to choose differently. It's another chance to walk away, to break free, to say, "I refuse to go back." And I won't lie to you: it won't be easy. The pull of the past is strong. The people who once knew you in that life will try to pull you back in. They'll remind you of the money, the rush, the way things used to be. But they won't tell you about the sleepless nights, the betrayals, the fear that grips you when you hear sirens in the distance. They won't remind you of the friends you buried, the years lost, the family members who watched you self-destruct, powerless to stop you. They won't tell you that every moment you stay in that life, you're gambling with your future, your freedom, and your very soul.

I don't know who this is for, but I feel in my spirit that somebody needs to hear this: **DON'T GO BACK**. Don't let nostalgia trick you into believing that what almost killed you is where you belong. Don't let loneliness make you settle for a situation that God already rescued you from. Don't let fear of the unknown keep you trapped in a cycle of pain and regret. You were made for more. You were created for greater. And if you don't believe that yet, believe this: if God has given you the grace to walk away once, He will give you the strength to keep walking.

I know it's hard. I know the struggle feels overwhelming. But let me remind you: You are not alone. God sees you. He hasn't abandoned you. Even when it feels like you have no options, He is making a way where there seems to be none. You may not see it yet, but that doesn't mean it's not there. You have to trust Him. You have to trust that the pain of leaving behind what's familiar is nothing compared to the peace of stepping into what God has for you.

I look back at my own choices, and I won't lie: there are days I wish I had done things differently. I wish I had invested that check in myself instead of a life that only took from me. I wish I had trusted that there was more for me than what I could see at that moment. But I can't change the past. What I can do is use my story to tell you: don't make the same mistake. If you have an opportunity to walk away, take it. If you have a chance to start fresh, don't hesitate. The streets aren't worth it. The pain isn't worth it. The regret, the loss, the wasted years: it's not worth it. But your future is.

If you're standing at that crossroads today, if you're debating whether or not to go back, I pray that you choose differently. I pray that you recognize the trap before you step into it. I pray that you see yourself the way God sees you: as someone worthy of a new beginning, as someone strong enough to break the cycle, as someone who is not defined by their past but by the God who holds their future.

So, this is my plea to you: don't go back. Whatever it is, whoever it is, however tempting it might seem, remind yourself of where that road leads. Remind yourself of the pain, the struggles, the nights you swore you'd do anything to escape. And then, remind yourself that you don't have to go back there. You are stronger than you think. You have more options than you believe. And most importantly, God is with you.

Walk away while you still can. Run if you have to. Whatever it takes, just don't go back. Because what's ahead of you: the life you haven't even imagined yet is so much greater than anything you're leaving behind.

REFLECTION

1. What specifically draws you back to your past, and what need is it trying to fill in your life right now?

2. When you think about going back, what emotions rise to the surface: fear, comfort, shame, loneliness, anger?

3. What would it cost you mentally, spiritually, emotionally, and physically if you went back?

4. What have you already survived and overcome, and how does that remind you of God's grace in your life?

5. Who in your life can you be fully honest with about your struggle to not return to old habits or environments?

6. Are you willing to be uncomfortable in your healing in order to stay free? Why or why not?

7. How has your past distorted your view of yourself, and what does God say about who you truly are?

8. What are the patterns or triggers that make you most vulnerable to slipping back? How can you prepare for them?

9. What healthy habits or support systems can you put in place to anchor you when you feel like giving up?

10. How would your future look if you chose healing over returning to the familiar pain of your past?

11. Who is watching your journey (family, friends, children, mentees) and how could your choice to move forward impact their lives?

12. What does it mean to you to cry out for help, and are you ready to do it consistently, even if you don't get the answer you expect right away?

CHAPTER SIX
UNCHARTED TERRITORY

LIFE ON THE NINE grew worse with each passing day. The violence intensified. Gunshots became an expected part of the night, and the silence in between was filled with dread. The police had us locked in their crosshairs, their presence becoming more aggressive and persistent. Sirens and searchlights became the soundtrack of our lives. It wasn't just heat anymore; it was a blaze, and we were burning in the middle of it.

People we once called brothers now looked at us with suspicious eyes. Friends became enemies, driven by envy, desperation, or fear. Jealousy filled the air like smoke, and we were suffocating. Loyalty was fading, turning to ash in the fire of greed. The very streets that had once embraced us now threatened to consume us. I couldn't sleep at night, not because I didn't want to, but because I couldn't. I was haunted by everything around me. The paranoia was real, and it crept into my thoughts like a thief, stealing my peace and rest. Every footstep behind me made my heart race. Every unfamiliar car that cruised down the block made my hand reach for my gun. I was exhausted physically, emotionally, and mentally. But the hardest part, the most unbearable pain, was watching my family slip. The drugs we sold, the same ones that put food on our table and money in our pockets, began to claim those closest to me. My own blood, now bound by addiction, became a tragic reflection of the very thing we were feeding. I saw the light leave their eyes. I watched their spirits become even thinner. And I didn't like that I was part of it.

I'd see teachers, businessmen, single mothers, teenagers, pregnant women (who I didn't allow my people to sell to): people from every background pull up, roll down their windows, and hand us their hope in exchange for their next high. I saw desperation in every hand that reached out, and something inside me began to ache. Was it guilt? Was it God? Or was it just the realization that I was meant for something more than this?

The question gnawed at me. I tried to push it away, but it kept returning: every night when I laid my head down, every time I saw my family getting high, every time I counted a stack of dirty money. Was this my destiny, or was this a detour?

The city had had enough. The Nine had become too powerful, too dangerous, and too much of a liability. The police formed a task force with one clear mission: destroy the Nine. Their plan was to arrest us and erase the very place we operated from. The buildings that had served as our headquarters, our refuge, our battlefield became targets.

The owner of the apartment complex lost everything, and the city wasted no time. Bulldozers roared to life, and brick by brick, they demolished the foundation of our empire. We stood there, watching the dust rise into the sky, as if our past was vanishing before our eyes. The Nine was no more. We were displaced, homeless in our pseudo-kingdom.

But the hustle didn't stop. It never did. We needed a new place to set up shop, a new street, a new corner, a new block to claim. I started selling weight: large amounts to keep the money flowing. But it wasn't the same. The Nine had been more than a spot. It had been a way of life. The connections, the control, the familiarity: it was gone.

That's when I ran into an old friend. He told me that Bloomington, Illinois, was ripe. The drug game was thriving there, unregulated, untapped. It was like a gold rush, and he encouraged me to make the move.

At first, it felt like a breath of fresh air. A chance to start over. The Nine was gone, but maybe Bloomington could be the next chapter. But it wasn't that simple. Bloomington was uncharted territory. I didn't know the people, the layout, or the rules. I didn't know who was connected, who was a threat, or who would try to take me out before I even got started.

Still, I was desperate. Money was drying up. The tension back home was unbearable. I felt like a king without a throne, a general without a war. I needed purpose. I needed movement. I needed to feel like I had control again.

So, I took the risk.

I packed my bags and headed to Bloomington. Everything in me knew this wasn't going to be easy. I was walking into a place where I had no history, no reputation, no allies. I was a stranger trying to carve out territory in a land already claimed by others.

I was nervous, but I masked it with confidence. That's what the streets taught me. Show no fear. Walk like you own the block, even if you don't. Make them believe before they see the cracks.

Setting up shop in Bloomington was a different experience. The rhythm was slower, the clientele was different, but the danger was the same. I had to move carefully, watch my every step. I had to rebuild connections from scratch, make deals, and establish a network. It was draining, but I was used to the grind. What I wasn't used to was the silence. Bloomington didn't have the chaos of the Nine. At night, the streets were quiet, and in that quiet, I started hearing things I hadn't heard in years: my thoughts, my regrets, my conscience. I couldn't drown them out with sirens or shouting or the rush of a deal. I was forced to sit with them.

And they spoke loudly.

In Bloomington, I began to unravel. Slowly, but surely. I was still making money, still surviving, but inside, I was breaking. I was tired of looking over my shoulder. Tired of wondering if today would be the day everything came crashing down.

This was uncharted territory. I was stepping into the unknown, not just in Bloomington, but in myself. Who was I without the Nine? Who was I without the hustle? Could I be someone more than this? I didn't know the answer, but the questions were growing louder. And maybe, just maybe, that was the beginning of something new.

Because sometimes, God doesn't show you the entire path: He just gives you a glimpse. A stirring. A conviction. A moment where you realize that what's familiar isn't necessarily what's best. And uncharted territory, as frightening as it is, might be where your deliverance lies. I was still in it. Still trying to figure it out. But something inside me was shifting. Slowly, painfully, but unmistakably. The grace I didn't think I deserved was following me, even here, even now.

This wasn't the end. It was a crossroads. And for the first time in a long time, I was starting to believe that I didn't have to keep walking the same road. Maybe there was another way. Maybe grace was calling me to it. Maybe this uncharted territory was where I'd finally find freedom.

A PLEASANT SURPRISE IN AN UNEXPECTED PLACE

I set up shop in Bloomington, and just like my friend said, the rhythm picked up fast, and the money? It flowed in even faster than I ever imagined. But Bloomington was different. It wasn't like Chicago. The noise, the chaos, the constant paranoia of drive-by shootings or rival beefs: it didn't exist here. It was quiet. Peaceful. A kind of peace I wasn't used to but found strangely comforting. There was no fear of violence, no jealous eyes watching your every move, no one scheming behind your back. Even the others from Chicago who made their way down here to set up shop seemed to operate under some unspoken code: no drama, no fighting over territory. It was, oddly enough, a kind of free enterprise.

The neighborhoods were clean. Their version of the projects looked more like townhomes tucked in nice areas of the South Side back home. And no one claimed ownership. No gang marked their territory. There was a freedom in that, something unfamiliar but refreshing. It didn't feel like a trap. It felt like potential. The city still had its shadows, its own dark side, but on the surface, it was calm. Controlled. I found a beautiful townhome on the far side of the city. Tucked away, quiet, and secure. It was far enough from my street operations to keep my family safe. So, I moved my girlfriend down there, pregnant with our second son, and I felt like I was finally doing something right. I had carved out a new space. A new life.

Bloomington became my second home. And as the money kept rolling in, I started making friends: some from back in Chicago, others new faces. We'd often meet up at a local tavern called Third Ward. That place became our social hub, but also a base for handling business. It was low-key, familiar, and safe. When I wasn't running things, I tried to explore the city more. One of my favorite pastimes became playing basketball. I'd hit up the local YMCA almost daily. It kept me grounded, helped me breathe.

It was there, on that court, where I met a man named Doty. He noticed my game right away and approached me after one session. "You can really play," he said. "Ever thought about playing organized ball again?" I laughed it off at first, but he was serious. He told me he ran a traveling team that competed against colleges all over the state. The idea intrigued me. Something in me, maybe the younger version of myself, lit up. I had always dreamed of playing at every level, of having people cheer from the stands while I put on a show. So, I said yes. I joined the team. Even though I was still knee-deep in the streets, this gave me another taste of a different life.

Bloomington sat right next to Normal, Illinois, the home of Illinois State University. I had friends from high school who went there. One weekend, we threw a huge party just down the street from campus. That night, a college kid walked into the party and invited us to another one the following weekend: a Kappa event. He mentioned there'd be a dice game, and naturally, that got my attention. I was always game to make a little extra money.

But what happened at that party caught me completely off guard. It wasn't the dice. It wasn't the music or the people. It was the environment. The way those students carried themselves. The sense of purpose. The community. I looked around and thought, "This is what I missed?" Seeing how those college kids lived and moved, hearing them talk about classes, internships, relationships, and dreams, I fell in love with the idea of college. I wasn't jealous. I was inspired. It lit something inside me that I thought had died a long time ago. I should have been here. I should have walked this path.

But I wasn't. I was still in the streets. Still slinging. Still counting money behind the scenes.

Then came a moment I'll never forget. Our traveling team was scheduled to scrimmage against Parkland College, a junior college in Champaign. I went in like I always did, ready to play hard, but this time with more heart. I wanted to prove something. Not just to them, but to myself. I played one of the best games of my life. When it was over, the coach pulled me aside. He offered me a partial scholarship. He said he saw potential. He said I belonged.

And just like that, I had a way out.

A real chance. Not a fantasy. Not a what-if. But an actual opportunity to start over. To do something different. Something meaningful.

And I couldn't help but wonder, was this God? Was this His way of reaching into my mess and pulling me out? Of saying, "You've had enough of the streets. Here's something better."

The streets had always felt like a one-way ticket. Once you were in, you stayed in until you died or got locked up. But now, here was this door. Cracked open. Inviting me in. I had a choice to make. Would I keep running with the streets or walk into the unknown?

The duality of my life was tearing me apart. On one hand, I had stability, money, and respect in the streets. On the other hand, I had a shot at redemption. At legacy. At purpose. And even though I didn't have all the answers, even though I was still confused and torn, I started to believe that maybe, just maybe, God hadn't given up on me. Maybe He was trying to reroute my path. Maybe all those nights I lay awake, staring at the ceiling, feeling the weight of the life I was living... maybe those moments were Him whispering, "There's more."

The question wasn't whether I could do it. The question was whether I would.

I wanted to believe the answer was yes, but the truth is, belief doesn't erase bondage.

I enrolled. I joined the team. I showed up at practice. But I was living a double life. By day, I was wearing a jersey, trying to play ball and go to class. By night, I was still knee-deep in the hustle, still chasing money that came with too many strings and even more scars. I told myself I could do both. I told myself I was in control. But the truth is, I was breaking.

In the classroom, I struggled. Not just academically, but mentally, emotionally, and spiritually. My mind was cloudy, like I was stuck in a fog I couldn't shake. I'd sit through lectures, unable to absorb anything. The guilt, the weight, the unfinished chapters in my life: they followed me everywhere. I was sitting in new spaces but carrying old pain. I wanted the freedom of a new life, but I hadn't divorced the systems and survival patterns of my old one.

I was assigned to an apartment with other players, but I barely stayed there. My body would return to campus, but my loyalty was still tied to Bloomington. The streets still felt like mine. I still had product moving. I still had people depending on me. And if I'm honest, part of me still needed that street validation. Still needed to be "him." Still needed to feel powerful, even while I was crumbling inside.

What started as relief, this escape from Chicago, this quiet city, this opportunity, started to feel like a burden I wasn't built to carry. I was trying to force my past and my potential to live in the same house. But oil and water don't mix. Peace and poison can't co-exist. One will eventually drown the other. And yet... through it all, I still found joy in practice. The court was still my sanctuary. In those moments, sweating, hustling, grinding, I felt like me again. Not the version the streets created. Not the version the system tried to contain. But me. The kid who once dreamed of doing something with his life. The boy who loved the game before he learned to love the game of survival.

Looking back now, I see it clear as day: God was giving me a glimpse.

Not the full picture. Not the whole promise. But just enough light to show me what was possible. He was saying, "Son, this is what it could be. This is the life you could have. But I can't give you the new while you're still clinging to the old." And He was right. There were still chapters in my story that I hadn't closed. Still loose ends. Still unpaid consequences. Still, soul wounds that hadn't been healed, just hidden. I was trying to build a new future on a broken foundation. But God doesn't bless who we pretend to be: He blesses who we surrender to become.

That partial scholarship wasn't just a reward for my game; it was a lifeline from Heaven. A crack in the concrete. A window in the prison I had built around myself. I knew it then: this was more than chance. This was divine intervention. This was grace. And yet, I wrestled. I wavered. I slipped. Because liberation doesn't come all at once. It comes in stages. Grace meets us in process. But here's what I know now: God wasn't afraid of my mess.

He didn't flinch at my failures. He wasn't intimidated by the weight of my street past. He loved me through it. He pursued me in it. He came after me, not when I was clean, but when I was dirty. Not when I was free, but when I was chained.

That's the kind of grace that breaks generational curses. That's the kind of grace that says, "Not guilty," even when all the evidence says you are. That's the kind of grace that doesn't just offer escape: it offers transformation.

REFLECTION

1. Where in your life have you been trying to straddle two worlds: your past and your potential? What is that doing to your soul?

2. Have you ever mistaken survival for success? In what ways have you convinced yourself that you were "winning" when you were really just coping?

3. What are the unfinished chapters in your life that you keep avoiding but know need to be closed?

4. Do you find yourself returning to familiar places or habits, even when you've been offered a new beginning? Why?

5. In what areas of your life are you trying to carry old patterns into new opportunities, and is it working?

6. Can you recognize moments in your past where God gave you a glimpse of something greater, even if you didn't fully receive it at the time?

7. What do you believe disqualifies you from grace, and is that belief rooted in God's truth or your own shame?

8. Have you ever felt God whisper, "There's more," in the middle of your mess? How did you respond to that whisper?

9. What does the idea of "liberation" mean to you, and what would it take to truly walk in that freedom?

10. Are you more comfortable in the chaos you know than in the peace you don't understand? Why does peace sometimes feel unfamiliar or even frightening?

11. What does it look like to surrender, not just your behavior, but your identity to God's grace?

12. If God isn't afraid of your mess, what's stopping you from bringing it all to Him right now?

CHAPTER SEVEN

WANTED ALIVE BUT DEAD

BLOOMINGTON STARTED LIKE A FRESH WIND, the streets were quiet, the money was fast, and the illusion of control was present. I had carved out a lane that felt safe, profitable, and low-key. It was a far cry from the chaos of Chicago. The money came in fast and hard. I was living good. I had a new townhome, my family close, and a second life as a ball player, trying to turn dreams into something real. But like the old saying goes, "More money, more problems."

I was walking on two roads in opposite directions, one toward purpose, the other toward prison. I was still trying to play basketball, still enrolled in school, but all the while managing street operations that were growing beyond my reach. And that conflict started ripping me apart from the inside out. The deeper I went into the hustle, the louder the streets got, and the more peace I lost.

The police caught wind of our operation and began moving in silence. Undercover agents began using all types of surveillance to watch us. I could feel it. The tension thickened with every move I made. They weren't coming loud and wild. They were building something strategic. They were coming for us methodically. They were even trying to use people close to us. One old friend was caught with a listening device in his pager. Then came the call that sent chills down my spine.

My mother phoned me in a panic and informed me that detectives from our hometown in Markham, Illinois, had shown up at her house with a warrant for me. I was being accused of a crime I didn't commit. A setup. False charges. But none of that mattered in the eyes of the law. My name was on that paper. My face was in the system. And my past was beginning to swallow my future. And just when I thought it couldn't get worse, I found out Bloomington PD had put together a full-scale case called *Operation Southern Passage.* I wasn't just on their radar; I was one of the main targets. I had unknowingly become a face on a wall, part of a web they were weaving to take me down. The walls were closing in. And fast.

They raided homes. Snatched up people I knew. People close to me. People who knew my name, my habits, and my family. And all the while, I was still showing up to class, still trying to wear the face of a student-athlete, pretending like everything was normal. Until the day everything changed. I was walking out of class and spotted a Bloomington Police squad car parked in the lot. It was just sitting there, but I knew. They weren't there for lunch. Something in me snapped. I couldn't risk it, so I walked away from that campus and never looked back. My basketball dreams were shattered in that parking lot. Gone. Just like that. And so, I ran.

I packed up everything I could, moved my family back to Chicago, and went underground. I was now officially on the run. Wanted in two cities. One case I had nothing to do with. Another that was built around what I did. It felt like the walls of every decision I ever made were caving in all at once.

I was a fugitive. A ghost. A shadow in my own life. But what I didn't know then was that God's grace was stripping me. Not to shame me, but to save me. He was breaking everything I built in my own strength so He could rebuild me in His. He was removing every false foundation, every fragile identity, every idol I clung to so that I could see the only thing that truly remained: Him.

I was wanted alive, but I felt dead on the inside.

The pressure was unbearable. I lived by the seat of my pants, always looking over my shoulder, always ducking into the shadows. The fake ID in my pocket might have fooled the world, but it couldn't protect me from the pain of the real me. The me that was broken. The me that was scared. The me that was tired of running.

I was losing it all. I burned through money like it grew on trees, trying to numb myself, trying to buy peace. But peace isn't for sale when your soul is bankrupt. I had no stable place to stay. No more cities to hide in. No more streets to work. I was a nomad, carrying shame, fear, and regret like baggage on my back.

Paranoia was my roommate. I couldn't sleep. I couldn't eat. Every knock at the door made my heart race. Every siren made my stomach drop. Even in a crowd, I felt alone. Even with people around, I was isolated. I was surrounded, but I was still dying on the inside.

THE CHASE

Being on the run was more than just physical, it was spiritual, mental, and emotional warfare. Every day was a balancing act between paranoia and survival. Every knock, every car that slowed down, every unfamiliar face felt like a threat. I was exhausted. Not just in my body, but in my soul.

Eventually, I found an apartment on the East Side of Chicago in a neighborhood where I could lay low. No noise. No drama. Just shadows and silence. But life was hard, brutally hard. I didn't have the luxury of rest. I couldn't exhale. I slept with one eye open and my back always against a wall. I was alive, but I wasn't living. I was breathing, but I was buried. Fear had become my morning coffee and my midnight lullaby. Then came the day my running ended. It started like any other. I woke up early and decided to head out to Harvey, Illinois, to kick it with some old friends. I didn't think much of it. The skies were clear, and the air was calm. I left my house keys at the apartment and told my kids' mother I'd be back later. I took my middle son with me, who was only three years old at the time, too young to know the storm that was brewing.

I spent the day hanging out with old friends, laughing, catching up, pretending like the past wasn't haunting me, and the future wasn't closing in. Then I called home. But the line was busy. I called over and over, but it was busy.

I couldn't understand why. My kid's mother had told me earlier that she was heading to the store, so I thought to myself, maybe she knocked the phone off the hook by accident. But still, something didn't feel right.

When I got back to the apartment, one of her friends happened to be arriving at the same time. She told me that she'd been ringing the doorbell, but no one answered. So, we stood there for a minute, casually talking. And that's when the unmarked detective car pulled up to the corner.

They didn't move. They just sat there, watching us. Her eyes shifted to me, and she said, "They look like they know you."

I smiled, calm as ever, and said, "Nah, they don't know me. They are probably looking for these guys that be hanging out around here." But inside, my heart dropped.

After sitting there for a minute, they turned down the street we were on, which happened to be a one-way and pulled into the alley next to us. I felt it before they even stepped out of the car, so I turned to her, handed her my three-year-old son, and said to her, "Take him with you. Now."

The detectives stepped out and asked me, "What's your name? Do you live here? Do you have any ID on you?"

I was ready and calm on the outside. I reached into my pocket and pulled out my fake ID with confidence. But as one detective examined it, something happened. He fumbled a paper in his hand, and for a split second, I saw it. My real face. My real name. My real warrant. I saw that they were there for me. My mind raced. And right then, I lied and said, "My mother lives upstairs. She's looking out the window right now." They looked up. And I ran. I took off down the street with my heart pounding and my legs pumping. The chase was on.

For thirty minutes, I ran through streets, alleyways, jumped fences, cutting through buildings. I was running for my freedom, or so I thought. But truthfully, I was still running from myself.

I finally ducked into a random apartment building. Adrenaline crashing. Sweat pouring. I knocked on a door, desperate. And then grace happened.

A stranger opened the door. A complete stranger. And they let me in. No questions. No hesitation. Just mercy in human form. I hid in the closet, heart slamming like thunder against my chest.

I could hear the detectives storming through the building. Knocking on doors. Yelling threats. The sound of boots, the sound of fists hitting wood, was getting closer and louder.

Then, the knock came to the door I was behind. They made threats. They said they'd force their way in. And the people who let me hide, they gave in. The door opened. The police rushed in.

They found me curled up in that closet like a child. Sweaty, scared, and done.

They cuffed me and walked me to the squad car. I collapsed into the backseat, my body spent, and my soul worn thin. But then something unexpected came upon me. Peace.

A wave of calm washed over me. Like a whisper saying, "It's over. You don't have to run anymore." I didn't understand it then, but I know now that it was God, wrapping His arms around me like a blanket in the cold. Covering me, even in handcuffs. He was speaking to me, even through pain.

Looking back, I realize that the open door to that apartment wasn't just a hiding place; it was a divine setup. God used them to open that door so I wouldn't die in the streets. So, I wouldn't go out in a blaze of pride or paranoia. He shielded me. He made a way for me to be apprehended without being destroyed. Because how many men do we know who ran, and didn't live to tell the story? That's God's grace. Grace doesn't always show up wrapped in comfort. Sometimes it shows up as a capture. As exposure. As an interruption. But it's all love. Because God will arrest you to rescue you. He will stop your flight, not because He wants to punish you, but because He wants to position you.

James Baldwin said, "Not everything that is faced can be changed, but nothing can be changed until it is faced." And in that moment, God forced me to face everything I'd been running from: my brokenness, my sin, my pride, my wounds, my identity.

God's grace will corner you until you stop hiding behind your own lies. He doesn't do it to shame you. He does it to save you. Because grace isn't just forgiveness, it's transformation. It doesn't just cover your past; it calls you into your future.

That day in the back of that squad car, I didn't know what was next. I didn't know how the story would unfold. But I knew one thing:

I was finally done running.

STOP RUNNING AND START FACING

If there's one thing I learned from my season on the run, it's this: you can't outrun what you need to overcome. You can change your city, change your number, change your name, but until you face what's broken, it will haunt every step you take.

Running may delay the consequences, but it doesn't erase them. It stretches the pain. It prolongs the inevitable. And often, it gives your problem power it doesn't deserve. That's what fear does: it hands authority to what God already promised He would give you the strength to conquer.

I was wanted, hunted, and trapped by my choices and haunted by my past. But in the back of that squad car, I learned something that changed me forever: *Freedom doesn't come from fleeing.* It comes from facing. That's why I need you to know, whoever you are, that whatever you're running from, you can't heal what you won't confront.

The Bible is full of people who ran... until they stopped and finally turned around in faith.

Remember Saul and the children of Israel? They ran from Goliath for forty days (1 Samuel 17:10-16). And the longer they ran, the more powerful he became. He mocked them. Intimidated them. Dominated their minds. That's what unaddressed problems do: they grow. They spread. They take over your thoughts and steal your peace.

But then came David, a young shepherd who didn't come with armor, but came with faith. He didn't run. He stood. And because he faced the giant, the giant fell (1 Samuel 17:45-50). That's what happens when faith confronts fear; victory breaks through.

And remember Jacob? He spent years running from Esau, fearing the consequences of betrayal (Genesis 27:41-45). But there came a day when God said, "You can't wrestle your way around this: you have to face it." And when Jacob finally stopped running and came face-to-face with his brother, what he feared never happened. Instead of revenge, he found reconciliation (Genesis 33:1-4). That's what happens when you face your past through the lens of God's promise; He meets you with mercy.

And who could forget the woman with the issue of blood? For twelve years, she suffered. For twelve years, she carried shame and isolation. But she stopped hiding. She stopped waiting. She pushed through the crowd and faced her issue, not just socially, but spiritually. She reached for Jesus. And in that one moment of faith, her years of pain met a Savior who had the power to make her whole (Mark 5:25-34).

Listen to me: what you're afraid to face might be the very thing God wants to use to set you free.

You're not alone. You're not hopeless. And you're not disqualified.

Yes, there may be consequences. But let me tell you something, the consequences don't compare to your freedom. The pain of facing it is temporary, but the peace on the other side is eternal. God won't always remove the consequence, but He will walk you through it and bring purpose out of it. So, stop running. Face it. Own it. Confront it. And do it with a faith that says, "I may be guilty of some things, but I'm not beyond grace." Because the God who called David, healed the woman, and reconciled Jacob is the same God who is calling you. And when you face what's been chasing you, you'll discover it was never stronger than the God who was waiting to deliver you.

REFLECTION

1. What are you currently running from emotionally, spiritually, or physically that God is calling you to finally face?

2. Have your attempts to escape your problems brought you peace, or have they only prolonged your pain?

3. Can you identify a moment in your life when you felt God's grace covering you, even in the middle of consequences? What did that feel like?

4. In what ways have your problems grown more powerful simply because you've avoided them?

5. How does David's willingness to face Goliath (1 Samuel 17:45-50) challenge you to step up and confront the "giants" in your own life?

6. What would reconciliation look like for you, as it did for Jacob and Esau (Genesis 33:1-4)? Is there someone you've been avoiding instead of confronting with grace and truth?

7. Do you truly believe that God's grace is strong enough to meet you in your mess and carry you through your consequences? Why or why not?

8. What fears are keeping you from stepping into the freedom God is offering you today?

9. What does the woman with the issue of blood (Mark 5:25-34) teach you about pressing through shame and disappointment to reach for Jesus?

10. Have you confused avoidance with faith? In what areas of your life do you need to stop running and start trusting?

11. When was the last time you felt a supernatural peace in the middle of chaos? Could it have been God reminding you He's still with you?

12. If you stopped running today and faced your truth with faith in God, what would be possible on the other side? What does true freedom look like for you?

CHAPTER EIGHT

THE CALM IN THE STORM

THE DETECTIVES PLACED ME in the back of the squad car and drove me to Bridgeport, Illinois, where I would spend the night in a holding cell before being transported to court the next morning. The silence in that car was deafening. My hands were cuffed, my future uncertain, and my heart was pounding like a war drum. The reality was setting in fast: I wasn't going home.

The cell was cold, plain, and lifeless like a tomb dressed in concrete. No pillow. No bed. Just a bench and the kind of quiet that forces you to wrestle with every mistake, every memory, and every ounce of regret you've been running from. I sat there in the quiet with the weight of everything I had done and hadn't done pressing down on me. I thought about my children. Their faces. Their laughter. I wondered how long it would be before I'd get to hold them again... if ever.

While I was sitting there, a police officer passed by my cell. He stopped and looked at me not with disgust or hatred, but with something close to compassion.

"How are you feeling?" he asked. I was too tired to fake strength. I told him, "I'm okay. I'm ready to put all this behind me."

He looked at me with a puzzled expression and said, "You don't seem like the type of guy who would be facing the charges you're here for. May God bless you. I hope it all works out for you."

I didn't realize it then, but looking back, I know now that was God's voice through a stranger. It was a divine whisper wrapped in human concern. God was calming the storm inside me before He allowed me to face the storm ahead of me. God met me there, even in a jail cell. But that calm was shattered the next morning. When I stood before the judge and I found out what I was really up against.

Attempted murder.

Home invasion.

No bond.

My knees didn't buckle, but my soul did. I stood there, nodding slowly, as if I understood, but the truth is, I was numb. I didn't commit the crime. I had no involvement. I wasn't even there. But the system didn't care about the truth. It only cared about names and narratives, and mine was smeared on both.

Then came the worst realization of all: I wasn't just facing charges in Chicago. I still had two open cases in Bloomington, and now I was buried under the weight of all three. The hope I had left was snuffed out with the judge's gavel. And just like that, I was placed on a bus headed straight for Cook County Jail.

It wasn't a bus; it was a rolling cage. A long school bus, retrofitted with cages over every window. A steel partition separating the guards from the inmates. Men shackled to each other like animals. No smiles. No laughter. Just stares, long, tired, broken stares, and the sound of chains rattling when we moved.

I stared out of the barred window, watching the world pass by as if I had already died and was being carried to my burial. And in a way, I was. My old life, the fast money, the street respect, the illusion of control, it was dying right there on that bus.

When we arrived at Cook County Jail, I felt the gates of hell open. Towers with guards. Razor wire on the gates, and solid steel doors everywhere. This wasn't a correctional facility. It was a pressure cooker for broken souls. And on the inside, processing was a nightmare.

They packed us into overcrowded holding cells. No space to breathe. The stench was unbearable. The smell of must, sweat, stale fear, and human waste filled my nostrils. People detoxing. Shouting. Crying. Rocking. Some praying. Some discussing their cases. Some completely lost in the fog of their high. The spiritual warfare in that place was palpable. I felt like an object on an assembly line. Stripped. Prodded. Searched. Branded with a new identity called Inmate.

They tossed us a bag lunch, if you want to call it that. A crusty bologna sandwich in a brown paper bag. It didn't taste like food. It tasted like defeat.

Eventually, I was issued jail clothes, baggy khaki colored clothing that hung off my body, and escorted to Division 1, the place that would become my new address. My new normal.

But even in all that darkness, something strange started to happen. Peace came over me.

I couldn't explain it. I was exhausted, angry, confused, and yet, there was a stillness in my soul I hadn't felt before. Not happiness. Not relief. But peace. A quiet calm, I now know that was the hand of God holding me together when everything else was falling apart.

As soon as I stepped onto the deck in Division 1, the atmosphere shifted. The energy was different. It was tense, watchful, and charged. It was survival of the fittest. Predators scanned for weakness. Eyes followed every move you made. The moment we were escorted in, a wave of questions came at us like heat:

"Where you from?"

"What are you?"

"Are you GD, BD, Vicelord, Black Stone, or a neutron?"

When I told them I was a GD (Gangster Disciple), the temperature changed. The tension dropped. The handshakes came quickly. They nodded in acceptance, introduced me to others who shared my affiliation, and just like that, I was "in." But what they saw as protection only reminded me of the broken brotherhood I'd been part of for too long. There was no real safety here. Only temporary alliances built on fear, false power, and unspoken rules.

I was assigned to a 6x9 cell: a steel box with barely enough room to stretch. Two bunks, a steel toilet, and a small sink to wash your hands, face, or brush your teeth. That was it. No privacy. No comfort. Just concrete, steel, and the sound of your own breath echoing back at you.

My cellmate was an older man. He nodded without much emotion, like a man who'd seen too much and felt too little. I dropped my small bag on the bunk, took a breath, and immediately made my way to the dayroom to call home.

As I stepped out of the cell, I heard someone say, "That's him."

I paused for a second, unsure. I didn't think much of it until I got to the dayroom and saw the TV. There I was. My face was plastered across the news. The headline read: "Fugitive Captured: Major Arrest in Fugitive Operation."

The reporter spoke of me like I was a legend. They talked about my name with weight. They detailed my capture as if I were some kingpin. They built a myth around me which added stripes to my "street cred" in the eyes of some inmates, but for me, it was a knife to the heart. Because I knew the truth. That screen didn't show the me who was tired, broken, and hurting inside. That broadcast didn't capture the real story, the man who wanted out, who wanted healing, who didn't want the crown they were putting on him. To the guys on the deck, it was honor. To me, it was another layer of shame.

I got on the phone, dialed the number, and when my kids' mother accepted the call, my voice was steady, but my soul was shaking. One of the first things I said to her was, "I probably won't be home for the next 10 to 15 years." No tears. No yelling. Just that same strange, indescribable peace. The kind of peace that didn't make sense. My kids' mother stayed quiet for a moment. I don't remember everything she said, I just remember the pain in her voice, and the lump in my throat I refused to let rise. I held back tears, not because I wasn't broken, but because I didn't want to show weakness to those who were still staring at me and eavesdropping on my conversation.

I ended the call. Sat in silence for a few seconds. Then turned to walk back toward my cell. But before I could make it back, something happened that shifted everything. A young man who couldn't have been older than 25 was standing in the corner of the dayroom with a small group of men. He looked over and asked, "You wanna pray with us?" I paused. I was tired. My head was spinning. My chest was heavy. But something inside of me said yes. I joined them. Right there in the middle of jailhouse chaos amidst the noise, the fear, the trauma, were a handful of broken men calling on God. And as soon as I closed my eyes, something shifted in me. I felt this surge of electricity, like a current rushing through my chest. The hairs on my arms and neck stood straight up. My heart pounded not in fear, but in reverence. My knees felt weak, but my soul felt strong. I didn't cry outwardly, but I wept inside like a man who had finally found home in the last place he expected. It wasn't emotionalism. It wasn't hype. It was God's presence, real, raw, and undeniable. And then came that peace again. Not the kind that numbs you. The kind that anchors you.

I stood there in the eye of the storm, accused, ashamed, confined, and yet I felt calm. I felt carried. Looking back now, I know exactly what it was. It was God's grace. It wrapped itself around me like a blanket in the cold. While everything around me screamed chaos, God whispered, "I'm still here." While the system called me a number, God still called me by name. It reminds me of Psalm 23:

"Yea, though I walk through the valley of the shadow of death, I will fear no evil: for Thou art with me." (Psalm 23:4)

That wasn't a metaphor for me. It was my reality. In that moment, I learned something about God I'll never forget: He doesn't need stained-glass windows or Sunday morning choirs to show up. He will meet you on a jail tier. He will walk with you into a 6x9 cell.

He will find you behind bars, with a broken heart and a damaged past. And He won't just comfort you, He'll begin to change you. That night, I didn't just meet other inmates. I met God. And I realized something I would carry with me forever: When the world closes in, God steps in. And where God steps in, hope rises.

Listen, don't ever let the enemy convince you that God doesn't love you. Don't you dare believe the lie that God isn't concerned about your life, your pain, or your future. I don't care how dark it gets, how far you've fallen, how many mistakes you've made. God sees you. God knows you. And God is in relentless pursuit of you. He doesn't wait for you to get it all together. He doesn't need you to clean yourself up before He comes close.

He will meet you right where you are, even if it's in a 6x9 jail cell, in the middle of brokenness, shame, addiction, or confusion. See, God doesn't always knock politely. He invades. He breaks through chaos. He walks into rooms where people have given up on you and says, "I'm not finished with you yet." Don't let your situation convince you that God has abandoned you. Your circumstances are not the final word—God is.

He showed up for me in a cage surrounded by concrete and steel. He spoke peace into a place filled with rage. He wrapped His presence around me when I should've been consumed by fear. And if He did it for me, I promise you: He'll do it for you.

That's what God does. He pursues. He protects. He preserves. So, when life feels like it's closing in. When guilt, shame, or regret tries to drown you, don't look down in defeat. Look up in faith.

REFLECTION

1. Have you ever mistaken God's pursuit of you as punishment instead of grace? In what ways might He be trying to get your attention right now?

2. What "cell" or confined place do you find yourself in emotionally, spiritually, or physically? How can you invite God into that space?

3. Have your circumstances ever caused you to doubt God's love for you? What would it look like to trust His presence even in the chaos?

4. Do you recognize moments in your past where God was trying to calm you before you faced something difficult? Reflect on what that calm meant and where it came from.

5. What lie has the enemy tried to make you believe about your identity? How does God's truth about you silence that lie?

6. Have you ever chosen false strength over honest vulnerability? What would change if you allowed yourself to be weak before God?

7. What does 'peace in the storm' mean to you personally?

8. Have you ever experienced God's peace when everything else was falling apart?

9. In what ways have you tried to run from your problems rather than face them with faith? What consequences have followed? What healing might begin when you turn to face them?

10. Like David with Goliath (1 Samuel 17:45-50), what giants are dominating your life because you haven't confronted them yet?

11. Are you ignoring God's presence in your life?

12. What would it look like to stop fighting God and start trusting Him in your current situation?

CHAPTER NINE

GOD'S PLAN

MY FIRST WEEK in Division One was a slow, painful unraveling of my present reality. The days were long. The nights felt eternal. Grief sat heavy on my chest like a weight I couldn't lift. I missed my children with a pain that words couldn't explain. I kept wondering if they were okay. If they missed me. If they were asking where I went, even though they were too young to understand what was happening. The reality of my choices had crashed into me like a freight train, and the echo of my past mistakes bounced off the steel and concrete that now surrounded me. But in the middle of my sorrow, something began to stir. That same young man who gathered inmates for prayer was holding a Bible study in the dayroom in the afternoon and evenings. He walked up to me and said, "Come on, brother. Pull up a seat." I didn't hesitate. I didn't make excuses. I just obeyed. Something deep inside me was pushing me. It was a force I now know as the Holy Spirit, who was pulling me into a moment I didn't even realize would change my life.

He opened up the Word with boldness and fire. As he spoke, I sat still, stunned. He looked me in the eye and said, "God wants to come into your life and change you, for His glory. There's a calling on your life." I wanted to believe it, but I didn't.

I couldn't imagine that a holy, powerful, righteous God would have anything to do with someone like me. My hands weren't clean. My heart was jaded. I was still gang affiliated. I figured I was disqualified from grace, but something inside of me was hungry for what he was saying. So, I kept coming. I kept sitting in that circle, surrounded by men society had written off, yet God was visiting us there. I started to feel something awaken in me. Not religion. Not rules. But a relationship. Then one day, right in the middle of bible study, the correctional officer called my name.

"Alston, you got a visit."

My heart skipped. Visits were gold. A lifeline. I thought maybe I'd see my kids, or their mother, just a sliver of normalcy. Something to give my heart a reason to keep beating.

I was escorted down to the visiting room. It was partitioned booths with stools, reinforced glass windows, and a steel circle in the middle of the glass punched with holes to speak through. As I walked past the stations, looking for a familiar face, I stopped dead in my tracks. It was my Aunt Theresa. I hadn't seen or talked to her since I was a little boy. There she was, sitting on the other side of the glass. I didn't know whether to smile, cry, or run. My eyes welled with tears, not just because of the joy of seeing her, but because I was ashamed. Ashamed she had to see me like this.

Then she leaned toward the glass and said, "Hello, Binky (my childhood nickname). I saw you on the news. And the moment it went off, God spoke to me and said, 'Go visit Chenier. I'm going to use him for My glory. I have a calling on his life. Tell him not to worry about what he's going through because I'm going to use it all to get glory for Myself. It's not over, so don't worry.'" Her words hit me like lightning.

How could God be this specific? This intentional? This near? I sat there, stunned. Tears welled up in my eyes, but I fought them back. I didn't want to break down crying in the visiting room in front of the inmates visiting with their families. But inside, something was breaking open. Then she held up a small piece of paper to the glass and said, "God told me to give you this scripture. Read it when you get back." I asked the officer for a pen, scribbled the scripture on a piece of paper, and we closed in prayer. Her presence radiated peace. She looked like an angel sent not just to visit, but to deliver a message from heaven. I walked back to the deck differently. Quiet. Heavy. Expectant.

I reached my cell, pulled out the Bible the leader of the bible study group had given me, and scurried through the pages looking for the scripture. And upon finding it, these words were recorded:

"For I know the plans I have for you," declares the Lord, "plans to prosper you and not to harm you, plans to give you hope and a future." — (Jeremiah 29:11 (NIV))

Everything around me faded. The noise, the tension, the steel, the shouting, it all vanished. And what remained were the words of God echoing in my soul. It was like time froze. I read the verse again and again, each time slower than the last. I dropped to my knees. I didn't have fancy words. No polished prayer. Just a raw, broken plea: "God... help me. And please forgive me."

Tears flooded down my face like a dam breaking after years of pressure. I didn't care who saw. But strangely, nobody came. Not my celly. Not the guards on patrol. It was as if heaven itself said, "Leave him be. This moment is Mine." It was sacred. It was holy. And in that jail cell, in that lowest place, God met me. His Word wrapped around me like a blanket. His presence flooded that small space like a tidal wave. And in that moment, I realized something was happening to me, through me, and around me that was strange, unfamiliar, and comforting at the same time. Something that wasn't out to destroy me but was out to redeem me. Something that wasn't punishing me, but something that was rescuing me.

As the days passed, God's plan for my life began to unfold in powerful and unexplainable ways. I was still attending Bible study faithfully. Every session became a sacred encounter. The Scriptures were now alive. The parables, the prophecies, the promises, they were personal. They were piercing. They were transforming me from the inside out. The more I leaned into God's Word, the more I felt Him leaning into me. I found myself speaking up, asking questions, and even encouraging others. Something was changing in me. Not gradually but supernaturally. I wasn't the same man who walked into that jail.

Then one day, my cellmate was sentenced and shipped off to prison. And just like that, I had the cell to myself; a 6x9 sanctuary where God was about to visit me again. It was quiet, and one day, while I was sitting on the edge of my bunk, reading, reflecting, something strange and unusual happened. A calm, yet thunderous voice spoke. A voice unlike anything I'd ever known. A voice that didn't come from outside, but inside that cell. The voice said to me, "Drop your flag and fear nothing, My son, for I am with you." I froze. I looked around the room. My heart pounded. My mind raced. Was I going crazy? Was someone messing with me? But then it came again, clearer, stronger, and more direct. It said again, "Drop your flag and fear nothing, My son, for I am with you."

I couldn't explain it, but I knew it was Him. It was the voice of God. Not condemning. Not harsh. But filled with divine authority and fatherly love. I didn't feel terror. I felt reverence. A holy stillness washed over me like a wave. I fell to my knees, not out of habit, but out of surrender. Tears welled up in my eyes and all I could say is yes.

The next morning, I got up with a conviction I couldn't shake. I walked straight to the two men who ran the deck for the GDs. These weren't just guys, they were gatekeepers, enforcers, decision-makers. And with a steady voice, I said, "I'm done. I'm dropping my flag."

One of them stepped forward, his face tightening with frustration. "That's not how this works."

And in that moment, fear tried to rise in my chest. My body tensed. I felt exposed. Vulnerable. But then right there in the middle of the tension, I heard that same voice in my spirit say, "Fear nothing, for I am with you." And before I even knew what I was saying, the words came flying out of my mouth with power and precision. I said, "Man, listen, Jesus was beaten and died for me. So whatever y'all gonna do to me, it doesn't compare to what He's already done for me. I'm out." I didn't plan it. I didn't rehearse it. It was straight from my soul, raw, real, and redeemed.

And then, what happened next was nothing short of a miracle. The leader looked me in the eyes, and said, "Man... I don't mess with God's people. You're free to go."

I was free! No "violation." No beatdown. No retribution. Just a release. In a place where loyalty to a gang could mean life or death, God stepped in and said, "This one belongs to Me." I walked away from that conversation a free man. Not just free from prison walls, but free from the bondage of gang identity, free from a life of destruction, free from a false sense of belonging that almost cost me everything. I no longer lined up with them. I didn't have to fight for them. I didn't have to represent that life anymore. I was free.

After that, I walked back into Bible study, I shared what happened, and the guys were overjoyed. That day, I realized something powerful: when God speaks, chains break, and His plan starts to unfold.

REFLECTION

1. Have you ever sensed God speaking directly to your spirit? If so, what did He say, and how did you respond?

2. What "flags" (identities, affiliations, or past commitments) might God be calling you to lay down?

3. Do you believe you're too far gone for God to use you? Why or why not?

4. How has fear or peer pressure kept you from stepping into the freedom God has offered you?

5. When was the last time you surrendered something completely to God, regardless of what others thought?

6. What does true freedom look like to you, not just physically, but spiritually and emotionally?

7. Can you recall a moment where God's peace showed up unexpectedly in your chaos? How did that moment shift your perspective?

8. Are you still trying to fit into spaces and systems God is calling you out of? Why are you still holding on?

9. Who in your life is encouraging you to walk with God, and are you listening to them?

10. How can you begin to surround yourself with people who point you toward purpose, not destruction?

11. Have you ever felt unqualified or disqualified by your past? How do you think God sees your story?

12. What is one bold, faith-filled step you need to take today to walk in the freedom and plan God has for your life?

CHAPTER TEN

NOT GUILTY

SOMETHING WAS HAPPENING TO ME. Each morning, I woke up with an eagerness I hadn't felt in years. Bible study had become more than a routine; it had become my refuge. I was hungry to learn, to grow, to share. Even though my knowledge of Scripture was limited, I found joy in contributing. My prayer life was deepening. My heart was softening. My spirit was waking up. But then the news hit us like a gut punch. The young man who had faithfully led our Bible study, the one who had poured into us day after day, was being transferred. His case had finally gone to sentencing, and he was headed to prison to serve his time.

Suddenly, the group felt adrift. I remember thinking, "Who's going to lead us now?" That question wouldn't linger long. One afternoon, after class, he pulled me aside. He looked me dead in the eye and said with quiet conviction, "God told me you're the one who's going to lead the study when I leave."

I froze. Fear gripped me. I didn't feel qualified. I didn't feel ready. I didn't know enough. I was barely learning how to walk in the Word myself. How could I possibly teach others? But deep down inside, there was a voice, gentle, steady, relentless, that was pushing me.

It wasn't my confidence; it was my calling that I wasn't fully aware of. I said, "I will do it." He told me I would start teaching while he was still there, so I could learn under his guidance. And just like that, another layer of God's mysterious plan unfolded in front of me.

"For I know the plans I have for you," declares the Lord...
(Jeremiah 29:11)

I sat in my cell that night, staring at the walls, overwhelmed by the weight of it all. I whispered, "Lord, I don't know enough to teach Your people." And before I could let

81

fear take over, God answered. A voice shouted from a few cells down. A man I barely knew. He wasn't even part of the Bible study. He shouted, "Hey, big man, open your Bible! I want to show you something." I was stunned. I grabbed my Bible and opened it. What followed felt like a seminary course in the middle of a jail tier. He broke down the Scriptures in ways I had never seen before. It was like God had assigned me a personal tutor behind bars. Heaven was training me in prison. When it was finally time to teach, I stepped up. Nervous, yes, but also anointed. And I loved it. The Word came alive in my mouth, and I saw light in the eyes of the men listening. I wasn't preaching from perfection; I was teaching from transformation. Grace had chosen me.

Then one afternoon, in the middle of teaching, a correctional officer walked in and said, "You have a visit."

It wasn't the assigned visiting day, so I was confused. As we walked, I noticed we weren't going to the normal visitation area. I asked where we were headed. "Attorney visit," the CO replied. "Your public defender is here." When I walked in, he stood to greet me, smiling like he had good news. He said, "I've got something great to tell you."

"What is it?" I asked, bracing myself for anything.

"The charges in Markham have been dropped. You're no longer facing the attempted murder and home invasion case."

I blinked, stunned. "How?"

"The State's Attorney reviewed the case, spoke to the victims, and determined you had nothing to do with it. You're free of that case." He smiled and added, "Congratulations. I know you still have some cases pending in Bloomington. I hope things turn out well for you."

I walked out of that room a free man, spiritually and legally. I couldn't stop praising God all the way back to my deck. That day, grace pronounced me "Not Guilty."

THE SYSTEM VS. GOD'S GRACE

We live in a country where the law says, "innocent until proven guilty." But for many men, especially Black men, that's a lie in practice. In reality, we're treated as guilty until proven innocent.

- According to the National Registry of Exonerations, over 50% of people wrongfully convicted and later exonerated are African American.
- Black Americans are seven times more likely to be falsely convicted of serious crimes than their white counterparts.
- Many of these wrongful convictions happen because of mistaken identity, corrupt witnesses, racial bias, and overzealous prosecution.

I was almost one of them. But grace stepped in. Grace found me in the shadow of a life sentence. Grace walked me out of that courtroom with my name cleared. Grace reminded me that man's judgment is never higher than God's purpose.

Hear me good: you may feel like your life has already been sentenced. You may feel disqualified by your past. You may even be carrying the shame of a crime you didn't commit, or one you did. But grace has the final say. It doesn't excuse your wrongs. It doesn't erase the consequences. But it declares that your past cannot cancel God's plan.

"So if the Son sets you free, you will be free indeed." —
(John 8:36)

That day in jail, I wasn't just cleared by the court; I was confirmed by God. And He's not done with me yet.

REFLECTION

1. Have you ever felt unqualified for something God was calling you to do? What stopped you from moving forward, or pushed you to say yes?

2. In what ways has fear tried to silence or disqualify your voice, your purpose, or your calling?

3. Can you think of a moment when God used an unlikely person to teach, guide, or encourage you? What did that reveal about how God works?

4. Have you ever mistaken your limitations for God's limitations? What would it look like to trust His power over your weakness?

5. Do you believe that your past disqualifies you from doing something meaningful for God? Why or why not?

6. What would it take for you to fully surrender and step into the role God may be calling you to, even if you're scared or feel unprepared?

7. Have you ever experienced unexpected grace in the middle of a hopeless situation? How did it shift your understanding of who God is?

8. How do you respond when people place labels on you based on your past, especially when God is calling you into something new?

9. When have you seen God's timing unfold in ways you didn't expect, but later realized were perfect?

10. Are you still carrying guilt or shame for something you've been forgiven for, or even falsely accused of? How can you begin to release it?

11. What areas of your life feel like a prison right now? Could those very places be the classroom where God is preparing you?

12. Can you declare, by faith, that God's plan is still at work in your life, even if you can't see the full picture yet?

MY JOURNEY TO FREEDOM

ONE THING I'VE LEARNED about the road to freedom is that it's never easy. In fact, it's one of the hardest, most soul-stretching journeys a person can take. And my own path was no exception. My journey to freedom was paved with uncertainty, burdened by past mistakes, but guided every step of the way by the invisible hand of God.

The day finally came for me to be transported back to Bloomington, Illinois, where the charges that still hung over my life were waiting for me. As I prepared to leave Cook County, the young brother who had handed the Bible study group over to me came up to me, looked me dead in the eye, and said, "Brother, when you get down to Bloomington, don't stop. Keep the Bible study going. Keep telling people about Christ."

I didn't hesitate. I looked at him and said, "Most definitely."

We embraced tightly, brother to brother, spirit to spirit and then the officer escorted me downstairs, where two sheriff's deputies were waiting. They shackled my hands and feet, binding me in chains that clinked and clattered with every step. My walk was reduced to a slow shuffle, more like a scoot than a stride. And just like that, the journey began.

The bus was quiet, smooth, and peaceful. The deputies were surprisingly kind. Talkative. They didn't treat me like a number, or like the monster my charges tried to paint me to be. For two hours, we drove through open farmland, passing cornfields and wide skies. I sat there, not free yet, but closer than I'd ever been. Then something happened that I will never forget. The officers pulled over at a Wendy's to get lunch. Now I don't know if that was standard procedure or not, but what I do know is God touched their hearts. They didn't just feed themselves. One of them opened his wallet and bought me a cheeseburger. I hadn't tasted food like that in months. And in that moment, I saw favor in the small things. Mercy in a meal. Even in shackles, God was showing me that His grace never left me.

When we arrived at the McLean County Courthouse, I was escorted into the courtroom, still shackled, surrounded by officers like I was some kind of kingpin. I wasn't. I was just a man, flawed, fallen, but fighting to rise again. The judge read the charges as such:

> CASE 1: Calculated Criminal Drug Conspiracy, Drug Conspiracy, and Narcotics Racketeering.

> CASE 2: Operation Southern Passage: Calculated Criminal Drug Conspiracy, Narcotics Racketeering, and Obstruction of Justice.

As the words hit the air, they also hit my chest. Heavy. Real. No matter how far I had come spiritually, I still had consequences to face naturally. Once the bond was set and the formalities were done, I was remanded and taken to McLean County Jail to await the next phase of my legal journey.

Unlike Cook County, McLean County Jail felt calmer. It wasn't overcrowded. The cells weren't soaked in the stench of despair. The holding cell wasn't filled with dozens of angry men yelling over each other. There was space. There was quiet. And as always there was peace. The food was better than the brown bag horror experienced during intake at Cook County Jail. The intake process was smoother, cleaner and more humane. And sitting in that space, waiting to be assigned a unit, I had time to reflect on something bigger than charges and chains. I thought about what freedom really meant. Freedom is never free. That's true in the physical. That's true in the spiritual.

I was learning that the road to freedom will cost you your comfort, your pride, your illusions of control. It'll force you to deal with the mess you've made. But it will also open the door for God to heal what you can't fix on your own. I thought about Joseph who was sold into slavery, falsely imprisoned, forgotten in a dungeon (Genesis 37-41). His road to freedom was long. But it led to purpose.

I thought about Moses and how he fled Egypt and wandered in obscurity for 40 years before being called back to face Pharaoh and lead his people to freedom (Exodus 2-3). His path was hard. But it led to deliverance.

I thought about Jesus and how He walked the road to Calvary, carrying a cross He didn't deserve, so we could walk in the freedom we don't deserve (John 19). That road led to resurrection.

Freedom is never easy, but it's always worth it.

To you who is reading this right now and you're wrestling with the consequences of your own choices. Maybe you're in a jail of your own: physical, emotional, mental, or spiritual. Hear me when I say this: Do not put yourself in a position to lose your freedom, because the road back is long, hard, and uncertain. Don't take your liberty for granted. Don't treat your peace like it's disposable. Value your choices. Honor your future. But if you do find yourself bound, know this: *God walks the hard road with you.* He doesn't wait at the finish line. He steps into the mess, into the courtroom, into the shackles, and He walks with you. Sometimes He even buys you a cheeseburger through the hands of a stranger, just to show you He's still present.

I was a man in chains, learning how to be free. Not just free from jail, but free from guilt. Free from shame. Free from the identity that the streets tried to stamp on my soul. And every mile on that road was a mile toward purpose.

"So if the Son sets you free, you will be free indeed." — (John 8:36 (NIV))

REFLECTION

1. What does "freedom" look like to you right now? Is it physical, emotional, spiritual, or all of the above?

2. Have you ever taken your freedom for granted?

3. What decisions or behaviors in your life may be threatening your freedom today?

4. When was the last time you recognized God's favor in a small, unexpected moment, like a kind word, a meal, or a stranger's kindness? How did it make you feel?

5. Can you think of a time when God used unlikely people to show you He was still with you, even in hard circumstances? How did that affect your faith?

6. What chains (habits, relationships, thought patterns) are currently keeping you from walking in full freedom?

7. Are you ready to surrender them?

8. When you heard about the charges being read against me, how did you feel?

9. Did it cause you to reflect on the weight of your own past or mistakes?

10. What does the story of Joseph, Moses, or Jesus teach you about endurance through difficulty on the way to freedom? Which one resonates with you most right now?

11. Do you believe God has a plan for your life, even when things look chaotic?

12. What is God trying to teach you in your current season?

CHAPTER TWELVE
THE MISSION FIELD

AFTER THE CHARGES AGAINST ME were read and I was processed into McLean County Jail, I was escorted to what would become my next temporary place of confinement. But unlike the chaos of Cook County Jail, where steel bars slammed and spirits broke, I was sent not to a tier, but to a pod. And from the moment I arrived, I could feel something in the air was different.

The pod wasn't just physically cleaner, it was spiritually quieter. There was no barrage of questions about gang affiliations, no territorial tension, no immediate need to prove or protect myself. In fact, the men already knew who I was. The local paper, *The Pantagraph*, or as many called it, The Slandergraph, had published a damaging article about me. My name was in the headlines, but my heart was still in God's hands. But here's the thing: even though the paper tried to define me, I knew that God was refining me.

The setup in the pod was far better, single-man cells with decent beds, a desk, a chair, and a private toilet and sink. But more than the material difference, my mentality had shifted. When I first walked into Cook County Jail, all I saw was a wilderness of fear, despair, and hostility. But when I stepped into McLean County, I saw more than a prison; I saw a mission field.

Now, theologically, I didn't fully understand what a mission field was back then. But deep in my soul, I felt the fire of purpose rising. I came with intention. I came with conviction. I came with the gospel. The words spoken to me by the young brother back in Cook County echoed in my spirit, "Don't stop. Keep the Bible study going. Keep telling people about Christ." And that's exactly what I intended to do.

After I was assigned a cell, I dropped off my belongings, fell to my knees, and prayed. Then I walked straight to a group of brothers sitting in the dayroom. They greeted me with a mixture of curiosity and respect. I cut straight to the point. "Do y'all have a Bible study here?"

They said no. There was a weekly church service and occasional visits from a chaplain, but nothing regular in the pod. Nothing consistent. Nothing real. That was music to my ears.

I immediately shared my testimony of how God met me in Cook County, how He called me out of gang life, and how He spoke to me in my cell. I told them I wanted to start a Bible study right here in the pod. Some of the brothers nodded with fire in their eyes. They were hungry. Not just for freedom but for truth. For hope. For God. That first night, ten men showed up. Ten.

We didn't have a pulpit. We didn't have robes or stained glass. But we had a Word from the Lord. And when God's Word goes forth, it never returns void. By the end of the study, six men gave their lives to Christ. Six souls were snatched from the grip of darkness and introduced to the light of God's grace. Right then, I realized something profound: God had taken a place of confinement and transformed it into a place of commissioning. What looked like a cell to others, God made into a sanctuary. What was designed to break me became a platform to build others. His grace didn't just cover me; it converted my thinking. McLean County Jail became my mission field.

So let me say this to every person reading this: never let your context cancel your calling.

You may be in a place right now that feels dark, unfair, lonely, or even shameful, but don't you dare let your current condition rob you of your eternal commission. Purpose isn't confined by prison walls. Destiny is not delayed because of disappointment. And the grace of God is not intimidated by your surroundings. God specializes in showing up in hard places.

Ask Joseph. He was betrayed by his brothers, falsely accused by Potiphar's wife, and thrown into a dungeon for a crime he didn't commit. But in that dungeon, God gave him dreams, wisdom, and favor. By the time Joseph came out, he wasn't bitter; he was better. He told his brothers in Genesis 50:20, "You meant it for evil, but God meant it for good." What looked like confinement was really refinement. The prison was preparing him for the palace.

Ask Daniel. He was exiled in Babylon, thrown into a den of lions for refusing to bow. But because he stayed faithful to God, the king couldn't sleep, the lions couldn't eat, and the people couldn't deny that the God of Daniel was real. His loyalty in captivity turned the king's heart toward God (Daniel 6:25-27). His context didn't cancel his witness; it confirmed it.

Ask Paul and Silas. They were beaten, bloodied, and shackled in a Philippian jail. But they didn't let their bruises bind their belief. At midnight, they started praising. They turned a prison into a pulpit, a cell into a choir stand, and God shook the whole jailhouse. Doors flew open. Chains fell off. And even the jailer got saved (Acts 16:25-34). That wasn't just deliverance, it was a divine assignment.

So, I dare you, child of God, to lift your eyes above your circumstances. Don't wait for the situation to change before you start serving. Don't wait for freedom before you start walking in favor. Wherever you are, God can use you. Right there and right now. Whether it's a jail pod, a hospital room, a broken home, or a weary heart, you are not disqualified. Your mess doesn't scare God. He'll meet you in your mess, transform it into a message, and send you back in with power and purpose. What you thought was a punishment might actually be your platform. So don't curse your context; consecrate it. Don't despise the season; declare the Word in it. God may have placed you there not to punish you, but to position you so others might see the light through your life. Because when you show up with faith in a dark place, that place doesn't stay dark for long. You become the light. You become the hope. You become the messenger. And just like He did for me in that jail cell, He will turn your prison into a mission field.

REFLECTION

1. Have you ever experienced a season where your surroundings felt like a prison? How did you respond to that environment?

2. In what ways might God be calling you to see your current situation not as punishment, but as a platform?

3. Do you believe that your pain has a purpose? How might God be using it to shape your calling?

4. What dark or difficult place are you currently in that you can begin to see as a mission field?

5. When was the last time you let your context define your calling instead of letting your calling transform your context?

6. What can you learn from Joseph, Daniel, Paul, and Silas about serving God in uncomfortable or unjust situations?

7. Have you ever led someone to Christ in an unexpected place or during a difficult time in your life? What did that experience teach you?

8. Are you more focused on asking God to take you out of your situation, or asking Him how He wants to use you in it?

9. How has your view of ministry changed after reading this chapter? Do you now see ministry as something that can happen anywhere?

10. Is there someone in your current "pod" (your job, school, home, or community) who needs the light of Christ through you?

11. What spiritual disciplines (prayer, Bible study, worship) can help you keep your focus on purpose when you feel confined or discouraged?

12. How can you start today to shift your mindset from feeling confined to being commissioned by God right where you are?

DREAMS

WHENEVER I SHARE MY TESTIMONY, I do so without hesitation and without apology because it was nothing less than my Moses-at-the-burning-bush experience.

The only difference is that Moses stood before a bush engulfed in holy fire; I lay on a prison bed in the stillness of the night. My burning bush was not made of branches: it was the sacred sanctuary of my dreams. While the world slept, Heaven's gates swung open, and the God who spoke to Abraham, who thundered on Sinai, who whispered to Elijah... stepped into my darkness.

And He did not simply visit me. He revealed Himself. He did not merely call me, He commissioned me. And He did not stop at commissioning; He clothed me with His power.

THE EMPOWERMENT DREAM

The first dream came just before release from night lockdown. I was seated in a convertible car; no roof, no barriers, open to the heavens. Beside me stood a man in a priestly robe and clergy collar. His face was hidden in holy mystery, but His voice... His voice was thunder wrapped in comfort. He said to me, "Do not be afraid to fight the devil, for wherever I send you, My power is with you."

The moment those words left His lips, power fell on me: not as a flicker, but as a flood. It was electric, alive, consuming. My fists clenched tight, my eyes squeezed shut, and tears broke forth like rivers bursting a dam. I wasn't just hearing about God's power; I was filled with it.

When I woke, my fists were still clenched, my cheeks still wet. A light, unusual, almost weighty filled my cell. The sunlight poured in as though Heaven itself leaned in close. I dropped to my knees, trembling in reverence, pouring out thanks to the Almighty. And there, in that concrete chapel of a cell, I knew God had anointed me for war against the works of the devil.

Later that day, I told the chaplain, who agreed with what Heaven had already declared: God had placed His power on me for the assignment ahead. I didn't deserve it, but the God who delights in using the weak had chosen me to carry His strength into battle.

THE FAITH-INSPIRING DREAM

The second dream came a few days later like a divine sequel. Once again, the man in the priestly robe whose face was unseen stood before me, but this time in a church that had been transformed into an arena for a wrestling match. The rules to the wrestling match were simple: face the smaller wrestler first, and then, if you survived, face the giant wrestler.

Before the contest began, the man looked at me and spoke the very words of Jesus, "If you have faith the size of a mustard seed, you can speak to your mountains, and they will move."

I repeated the words back to Him, and as I did, an unshakable confidence filled me. But instead of fighting the small wrestler first, I walked straight past him and stood before the giant wrestler. He was massive, ugly, and terrifying, but as I squared up to fight, I woke up. Yet I woke up knowing I had won.

I sat on my bed, pondering. And it became clear to me that the small wrestler was my smaller case. The giant wrestler was my biggest case, the one they called Operation Southern Passage. Thirty people had already been convicted. I was the "top man." No one had beaten it yet.

From that moment, I began declaring what God had shown me: *I'm going to beat the case.* Inmates laughed. Others said I was crazy to take it to trial. But I had heard from Heaven, and faith like that doesn't bend.

Then the dream began to manifest in real time when I went to court to set trial dates for my cases. The judge asked the

Assistant Attorney General which case they wanted to try first. He said, "We'll try the big case first."

My attorney later said to me, "That was strange and unusual. I've never seen them do something like that. They usually start with the small ones."

Right there, in that holding cell, God's voice echoed, "Remember what I told you in the dream."

I saw instantly that the smaller case was the small wrestler. The big case was the giant wrestler. And just like in the dream, I skipped the small fight and went straight to the big one.

I hadn't even entered the ring of that courtroom battle yet, but by faith I already knew the outcome. God had shown me the victory before the fight. Because when Heaven speaks, you don't need to see the end to know how the story will turn out.

GOD STILL SPEAKS

From the very first words, "Let there be light," to the final "Amen" of Revelation, Scripture reveals an unshakable truth: our God is a speaking God. He is not silent. He is not passive. He is not distant. He speaks because He longs to be known. He speaks to unveil His glory, to reveal our identity in the light of His holiness, to clarify our calling, and to unfold the breathtaking plans He has for our future.

Throughout redemptive history, the divine voice has broken into human reality in countless ways:

He spoke to Moses from the burning bush (Exodus 3:4-6), revealing His holiness and His relentless plan for deliverance.

He called Samuel in the stillness of the night (1 Samuel 3:1-10), igniting a prophetic ministry in a boy while the nation slumbered in spiritual darkness.

He filled the temple with His glory before Isaiah, causing the prophet to cry, "Woe is me! For I am undone" (Isaiah 6:5), seeing both his sin and God's majesty in a single moment.

He interrupted Paul on the road to Damascus with a blinding light (Acts 9:3-6), transforming a persecutor into a preacher of the gospel.

He visited John in exile on Patmos (Revelation 1:9-19), pulling back the curtain to reveal the risen Christ and the hope of His coming Kingdom.

And to the weary and broken Elijah, hiding in a cave, He spoke not through wind, earthquake, or fire, but in a gentle whisper (1 Kings 19:11-12): reminding us that the truest encounters with God often happen when the world's noise is silenced.

But here lies the tragedy: many of us fail to hear God, not because He has stopped speaking, but because we have tuned our ears to lesser voices. The static of social media, the roar of cultural opinion, the replay of past regrets, the engagement of gross sin, and the volume of our fears all compete for our attention, which drowns out the still, small voice that is calling us home.

Yet there is one place where God speaks with unshakable clarity every single time: His Word. The Bible is not a dusty record of ancient speech; it is "living and active, sharper than any two-edged sword" (Hebrews 4:12), cutting through confusion and breathing fresh life into every generation. The psalmist declared, "Your word is a lamp to my feet and a light to my path" (Psalm 119:105). Paul reminds us that all Scripture is "God-breathed... useful for teaching, rebuking, correcting, and training in righteousness" (2 Timothy 3:16-17).

God's voice takes many forms: sometimes He thunders in power, sometimes He whispers in stillness. Sometimes He speaks through visions and dreams (Joel 2:28; Acts 2:17), through prophets and preachers (Jeremiah 1:9; Romans 10:14-15), or through divinely orchestrated circumstances (Genesis 50:20). And sometimes, He draws us back to the pages of His written Word where His voice is as alive today as when He first spoke it.

And here is the good news for your lowest moments: when you feel abandoned, He is still speaking. When grief steals your breath, He is still speaking. When shame tells you you're unworthy, His voice declares you redeemed. The God who whispered to Elijah in the cave is the same God who will meet you in the dark corners of your pain. He speaks not only to guide you out of the valley but to remind you that He is with you in it (Psalm 23:4). His voice cuts through the hopelessness, not merely to give instructions, but to restore your soul.

If you truly long to hear Him silence the noise, open His Word, bow your heart, and lean in. The Ancient of Days is still speaking. The question is not whether God speaks, but whether you are tuned to His frequency.

FIVE POWERFUL WAYS TO HEAR GOD'S VOICE

1. SILENCE THE COMPETING VOICES. You cannot discern the whisper of God while the roar of the world fills your ears. Create intentional moments of silence: turn off the phone, close the laptop, step away from the crowd and give your soul space to breathe. Stillness is not a luxury; it is a necessity for divine hearing (Psalm 46:10).

2. ABIDE IN HIS WORD DAILY. God's voice is most clearly heard through the Scriptures. Approach your Bible not as a textbook, but as a conversation with the Living God. Read slowly. Pray over the words. Let them read you as much as you read them. The more His Word saturates your heart, the more familiar His voice becomes (John 10:27).

3. PRAY WITH AN OPEN HEART. Prayer is not just speaking; it is listening. Ask the Lord to speak, then wait with expectation. Don't rush the silence after your "Amen." Many of God's greatest revelations arrive in the stillness after we have stopped talking (Habakkuk 2:1).

4. PAY ATTENTION TO HOLY NUDGES. God often speaks through gentle promptings: an unshakable burden for someone, a conviction to act, a sudden clarity about a

decision. Test every prompting against Scripture, but do not ignore the Spirit's quiet urging (Acts 16:6-10).

5. **SEEK GODLY COUNSEL.** God sometimes speaks through the wisdom of others who are anchored in His Word. Surround yourself with people who know Him, love Him, and are not afraid to tell you the truth in love (Proverbs 11:14).

REFLECTION

1. When was the last time you clearly sensed God speaking to you, and what was your response?

2. What noise (external or internal) is most likely drowning out God's voice in your life?

3. Do you truly believe that God still speaks today, or do you act as though His voice is distant and silent?

4. How often do you approach God's Word expecting Him to speak directly to your present situation?

5. In what ways have you ignored or resisted God's voice because it was not what you wanted to hear?

6. What can you learn from biblical examples (like Moses, Samuel, Elijah, or Paul) about responding to God's call?

7. Are you cultivating quiet, unhurried moments where you can discern God's whisper, or is your life too rushed?

8. Have you sought wise, Spirit-led counsel to help confirm what you believe God is saying to you?

9. In seasons of pain, discouragement, or confusion, do you lean in to listen for God's voice, or do you withdraw?

10. How might your view of God change if you recognized His voice in every circumstance, both in the spectacular and the ordinary?

11. What specific changes can you make this week to tune your heart more fully to God's frequency?

12. If God spoke something to you today that required courage and obedience, would you be ready to act?

FAITH ON TRIAL

THE DAY HAD FINALLY ARRIVED for me to face the big wrestler called Operation Southern Passage. The tension in the air was thick, like the moment before Goliath stepped toward David. We were set to pick a jury, but before the process began, my attorney approached me with an offer: 20 years in prison. Before he could finish his sentence, my spirit rose up, and I cut him off. "No. Let's pick this jury."

Choosing a jury was nothing short of frustrating. Faces from different walks of life, ethnicities, and ages sat before us. The process was a blur: questions, dismissals, replacements. But two people stood out in my memory like landmarks in a desert.

The first was a middle-aged white man. When the judge asked if anyone had an issue serving, his hand shot up. He spoke of urgent business matters and his desire to be anywhere but there. His face was a billboard of disinterest; his tone dripped with irritation. Yet, in an almost calculated move, the Assistant Attorney General selected him. Afterward, he glanced at me with a look I'll never forget, a glare that carried the unspoken verdict of his heart. My flesh said, This man will never be impartial.

The second was a young white man who also raised his hand when the judge asked if anyone could not be fair. His admission was shocking in its candor: "I can't judge fairly because I was raised in a prejudiced home and was taught not to like Black people."

He was dismissed immediately. As he walked past me toward the exit, he turned, looked me in the eye, and said, "Good luck, man. I hope everything works out for you."

My reply was simple: "God bless you, man. Thank you."

I respected his honesty because he could have easily remained silent, stayed on the jury, and used his prejudice as a weapon against me. His words were a whisper of grace from the throne of God, a reminder that the Lord can turn hearts and arrange even the smallest details for our good.

After twelve jurors were chosen, court adjourned for the day. The trial would begin in the morning.

The next day came, and I sat in the back, waiting to face the big wrestler again. My attorney walked in with another offer: this time, 10 years. I looked him dead in the eye and said, "No. We are going to trial, because God said He is going to deliver me from this case."

He smiled and said, "Let's go!"

Now, you need to understand, I didn't have a high-powered attorney. I had a public defender in a county with an 89% conviction rate for African Americans. My declaration was not rooted in legal strategy; it was rooted in divine certainty. It was a statement of faith that was confident, unshaken, and immovable.

At that moment, I realized something profound. It wasn't just me on trial, it was my faith. What I claimed to believe about God was about to be tested under the harsh lights of the courtroom.

And that's what life often does. Life will drag you into the courtroom of uncertainty and seat you before a jury of your fears, doubts, and circumstances. It will ask, "Do you still believe God is able?" Your faith will be on trial, and you will be interrogated about who and what you believe.

The bible teaches us that faith is tested in the furnace of affliction (1 Peter 1:6-7). Noah's faith was on trial when he built an ark with no sign of rain (Genesis 6-7). Abraham's faith was on trial when he climbed Mount Moriah with Isaac, not knowing how God would provide (Genesis 22:1-14). Daniel's faith was on trial in the lion's den (Daniel 6). The three Hebrew boys' faith was on trial in the fiery furnace (Daniel 3). And Elijah's faith was on trial when he faced the prophets of Baal on Mount Carmel (1 Kings 18).

Like them, I was being asked to walk into the unknown, guided only by the promise of God. And when faith is on trial, comfort is not guaranteed, but victory is promised.

So, to you who are reading this, do not surrender your faith in the dark. When your back is against the wall, when the odds are stacked against you, when the "jury" of life looks hostile, stand your ground. Faith will guide you through the shadows. Faith will steady you in the storm. Faith will remind you that your case has already been decided in Heaven before it ever hits the floor of the courtroom. Because in the end, it's not just about winning the trial in front of you, it's about proving that you trust the Judge who presides over all.

DAY 1

Day 1 of the trial opened with words that pierced like arrows. The Assistant Attorney General stepped forward, armed with a well-rehearsed script, and began to paint me as something I was not: a monster. In his version, I was a predator preying on the broken, a profiteer of pain, the orchestrator of a violent criminal enterprise flying under the banner of the Gangster Disciples. His accusations rang loud in the courtroom, but even louder in my mind. I wanted to stand up and shout, "That's not true!" Yet I sat still, knowing my voice would not be heard in that moment.

Looking back now, I realize that he was simply doing his job. He didn't know my heart, my story, my faith, or my God. He was speaking from his perspective, with the information he believed to be true.

But then, my attorney rose, and in that moment, he became my advocate. With integrity and honor, he dismantled the accusations, declaring that the so-called evidence was false. He was my voice when I couldn't speak for myself.

It was in that exchange that God taught me something: when your faith is on trial, it will be challenged by what you hear. The words of the prosecution echoed like the taunts of Goliath, attempting to intimidate and instill fear. And I must confess, fear and doubt tried to creep in. I could feel them at the door of my mind, knocking, hoping to be let in.

104

But when my lawyer spoke, I was reminded that the enemy will always release words that contradict what God has already declared over your life. The trial may take place in a courtroom, but the real battle is fought in your mind: between what you hear and what you know God has said.

It is the same in Scripture.

In Numbers 13-14, ten spies spoke words of defeat, while only two (Joshua and Caleb) held fast to God's promise. The people's faith faltered because they listened to the wrong voices.

In 1 Samuel 17, Goliath's daily threats demoralized Israel's army, but David refused to let the giant's voice be louder than God's.

In Luke 8:49-50, Jairus was told his daughter was dead, but Jesus said, "Do not be afraid; just believe."

The enemy's voice will always try to drown out God's voice. The question is: which one will you give the microphone to in your heart?

That day in court taught me this: the truth of God's Word must be the anchor in the storm of accusations. Because when your faith is on trial, it's not enough to hear God once—you must replay His voice again and again until it drowns out every lie, every fear, and every whisper of defeat.

DAYS 2-6

Days two through six of my trial were a furnace of affliction. The atmosphere in that courtroom felt like the fiery furnace in Babylon that was heated seven times hotter by lies, distortions, and venomous accusations. Six witnesses took the stand against me.

Before describing their words, it's important to understand the structure of this case. Like Nebuchadnezzar's towering statue that was built from different metals but standing as one, this case was pieced together from individuals, some of whom I knew casually, others I had never associated with at all. Yet together, they were assembled into one monstrous image that the prosecution bowed to as "truth."

One was a young white woman in her mid-twenties who claimed I had visited her home to broker large cocaine deals with her boyfriend, a member of a rival gang from Chicago's West Side. Her words dripped with confidence, but none of it was reality. I had never been to her home. Never sat with her boyfriend. I had seen her in passing, but our lives had never intersected beyond a glance. Still, there she stood, declaring fiction as fact.

Then came Big Jug. His testimony was a tapestry of falsehoods, claiming he had witnessed me supplying drugs on numerous occasions. That morning, before court began, something unusual happened. I was in a holding cell when they brought Big Jug in and placed him in the same room with me, something that should have never happened, especially with an active witness. I immediately alerted the officer, who looked as if he'd been caught in the middle of a plan. He quickly removed Jug. Even then, I could feel a trap being laid. Psalm 57:6 says, "They spread a net for my feet—my soul was bowed down. They dug a pit in my way, but they have fallen into it themselves." That verse became the lens through which I saw that moment.

Next came Chris, who was someone I considered a true friend. I had given him shelter when he had nowhere to go. Now, he stood in the witness box, hostile toward the prosecution yet unwilling to even look at me. His evasive answers and tense body language betrayed an inner war, and it grieved me to watch him be interrogated. I wanted to yell, "Leave him alone!" But I couldn't. It was like watching Peter in the courtyard, torn between loyalty and self-preservation.

Then there was an older white man whose name escapes me. His time on the stand was short, but his accusation was sharp, that I had supplied Chris with drugs to sell from his home.

The undercover agent followed, a towering man, 6'7", light-skinned, with piercing hazel eyes. He claimed he had seen me at a local nightclub called "After Hours," playing pool with other defendants on the case. The moment he spoke, I recognized him. I remembered seeing him sitting at the bar, pretending not to watch us, though his size and presence made

106

his disguise impossible. That fleeting encounter was the only "evidence" he had against me.

Finally, they brought in Lil Rob, a friend from grammar school. He had once been someone I laughed with in gym class, where a careless wrestling move had left me injured but laughing alongside him. Now, decades later, he entered as a government-protected witness, having turned informant in a high-profile case involving Larry Hoover. He wore a T-shirt that read "OUTLAW" across the front. With immunity in his pocket, he testified against me. I barely heard his accusations because my mind kept replaying our junior high memories, how we were once brothers in youth, now divided in adulthood.

When court adjourned, I was escorted back to my holding cell. Moments later, federal agents came for him. As he passed my cell, he looked at me with a smile and called out, "Man, why did you take that to trial?"

Without hesitation, I answered, "Because I'm not guilty and God said He is going to deliver me from this case." And then he was gone.

Those days reminded me that faith isn't only tested in what you see, it's tested in what you hear. The enemy's voice will always try to be louder than God's, just as Goliath's taunts echoed louder than Israel's faith, and just as Jezebel's threats tried to drown out Elijah's prophetic courage. But Elijah discovered in that cave that God doesn't always speak through the earthquake or the fire—sometimes, He speaks in the still small voice (1 Kings 19:11-12).

And that's the voice I had to cling to, above the accusations, above the lies, above the noise. Because when God has spoken a word over your life, every other voice becomes a counterfeit echo.

As I sat there, hearing each witness speak against me, I found myself wrapped in an unexplainable calm: a peace that could not be manufactured by human will. I was not mad. I was not bitter. I was not plotting revenge. In that moment, the Spirit of God revealed to me a profound truth: When your faith is on trial, the real battle is not about what is being said about you, but about what you believe and how you respond to what is happening to you.

The Scriptures make this plain in Luke 17:5, where the disciples plead, "Lord, increase our faith." Why did they ask this? Because just before that request, Jesus had taught them the radical, humanly impossible command of forgiving seven times seventy in a single day. Forgiveness is not a side issue; it is the acid test of faith. Faith is not merely believing in God; it is embodying what you believe about God. It is the lived reality of divine truth in the most unjust and painful moments of life.

So, I forgave them. all of them. Those who lied. Those who twisted the truth. Those who betrayed me. They were men and women backed into a corner, clawing for survival, trying to save their own lives. I understood their desperation.

Then came the moment that would test my words. After Big Jug testified against me, the state blindsided him with a suppressed warrant, charging him with another crime. He was locked in McLean County Jail, the same place I was housed. By "coincidence," they placed him in my unit. An officer, seeing the potential for conflict, grew visibly nervous.

I looked her in the eyes and said, "Don't worry. He can stay here." I reminded her of who I was now and how she had seen me lead Bible study week after week, pointing men to Christ, not chaos. She allowed him to remain.

That night, I walked over, greeted him, and invited him to join our Bible study. Before we opened the Word, we sat and talked. He apologized with sincerity. I told him, "I understand. You wanted to get back to your family. I have no right to hold this against you. If God has forgiven me for all I've done in my past, how could I dare withhold forgiveness from you?"

And right there, in the middle of a jail pod, the man who once testified against me, I offered God's plan of salvation to him, and he bowed his head and surrendered his life to Jesus Christ. My faith on trial had moved beyond mere words: it had been incarnated in action.

The streets have a code that says, "Snitches get stitches." But heaven has a greater decree, "Snitches get salvation."

So, I say to you, do not only have faith in what God has said, but live out what God has said. Let your life preach even louder than your lips. Because in the end, faith is not proven in the comfort of Sunday mornings; it is proven in the crucible of life's trials.

REFLECTION

1. When accusations and lies rise against you, whose voice are you listening to more: the voice of people or the voice of God? (John 10:27)

2. How has the enemy tried to redefine your identity through the words of others, and how have you responded?

3. Do you allow fear and doubt to creep into your heart when you hear something that contradicts God's promises for your life? (2 Timothy 1:7)

4. Are you convinced, deep down, that God has the final word over your life no matter what anyone else says? (Romans 8:31-34)

5. When your faith is on trial, do you stand firm on what God has already spoken, or do you waver under the pressure of people's opinions? (James 1:6-8)

6. How do you respond when someone wrongs you: do you lash out in anger, or do you walk in forgiveness the way Jesus commanded? (Luke 17:3-4)

7. What does the way you respond in your trials reveal about the strength and authenticity of your faith?

8. Have you realized that forgiveness is not just obedience to God but also a testimony of faith that others can actually see and experience?

9. How is God calling you to not just believe in Him, but to live out what you believe in visible, tangible ways? (James 2:17)

10. Is there anyone you've been holding bitterness against, and how might God be calling you to release that today?

11. Are you willing to be a vessel of grace, even to the very people who wronged you so that they, too, might experience salvation through Christ?

12. Do you believe that the very trial you are going through right now could become the testimony that leads someone else to Jesus? (Genesis 50:20; Romans 8:28)

CHAPTER FIFTEEN
NOT GUILTY

⎯⎯═◇◇◇═⎯⎯

DAY FIVE OF THE TRIAL came with the weight of the state resting its case. On day six, the attention shifted to my defense. My attorney made a bold choice: he only called one witness, me. I had to take the stand and testify on my own behalf. I can still feel the tension of that witness chair, the sting of cross-examination, and the unrelenting eyes of those twelve jurors studying every word, every glance, every expression.

Before I ever stepped onto that stand, my attorney prepared me. He told me, "When you answer, don't look at me, look at the jury. They need to see the sincerity in your eyes."

So, when he questioned me, he stood near the jury box, anchoring my attention on the very people who would hold my future in their hands. But when the state cross-examined me, the Assistant Attorney General strategically stood on the opposite side of the courtroom, forcing me to turn my head back and forth like a tennis match: questions served one way, answers returned toward the jury. Every response became not just my words but my testimony of truth and endurance.

When the sixth day ended, my attorney rested his case. On the seventh day, the judge gave instructions to the jury and sent them away to deliberate. By then, my body was drained. Every night after court, I would stumble back to my cell exhausted. I would collapse, pray, take a nap, and then rise again to teach Bible study to my fellow inmates. Even in the middle of my storm, the Word of God had to keep flowing. But waiting for the jury's verdict: that was its own battlefield.

To my surprise, the jury only took three hours to reach a decision. Three hours for seven days of testimony. Three hours to decide my future. When word came, my heart raced. The next day, I returned to court. I believed God, I trusted His Word, but I cannot deny the emotional war raging inside of me.

My family filled the courtroom, their nerves mirroring my own. My babies were there too, too young to grasp the moment, but old enough to make silly faces with me as I tried to calm my spirit with their laughter.

Then came the moment. We were told to rise as the judge entered. The jury filed back into the courtroom. My eyes locked on one juror, the man who showed displeasure about being there during the jury selection process. Yet, this time, he locked eyes with me, and with a subtle nod, gave me what I now recognize as God's silent reassurance that said, "Peace. What I promised is about to come to pass."

The foreperson stood. The judge asked the question: "Has the jury reached a verdict?"

"Yes, Your Honor."

We stood. My heart pounded. Then came the words that changed everything:

> "We, the jury, find the defendant, Chenier Alston, **NOT GUILTY** of Calculated Criminal Drug Conspiracy, Criminal Drug Conspiracy, Narcotics Racketeering, and Obstruction of Justice."

In that instant, joy erupted like a floodgate in my soul. Tears poured down my face. Behind me, my family broke out into shouts of praise. My attorney smiled and embraced me, but I knew: this wasn't just his victory. This was God. His fingerprints were all over the trial.

Though the dream I had prior cut off before I defeated the wrestler, I knew I defeated the wrestler, and in that courtroom, even though the verdict was not read yet, I believed I had already won. My mustard-seed faith was present during the trial, and it moved that mountain before me (Matthew 17:20).

I wasn't released that day; another smaller case still loomed, but I walked back into that jail with a new song. I shouted all the way through the halls: "NOT GUILTY!" When I reached my pod, the news had already spread. My brothers inside greeted me with cheers, handshakes, and hugs. We celebrated because the God who fights battles had shown Himself faithful again.

Looking back, I see the sovereignty of God woven through every detail. The trial lasted seven days. In Scripture, seven is the number of completion, perfection, and fulfillment. On the seventh day, God finished creation and declared it good (Genesis 2:2). On the seventh march around Jericho, the walls came tumbling down (Joshua 6:15-20). And after seven days of trial, God brought my case to completion.

And then, there were the three hours of deliberation. In the Bible, three is the number of resurrection, deliverance, and divine intervention. On the third day, Abraham lifted his eyes and saw Mount Moriah, the place of provision (Genesis 22:4). On the third day, Hosea declared, "After two days He will revive us; on the third day He will raise us up, that we may live in His sight" (Hosea 6:2). And on the third day, Jesus rose with all power in His hands (Luke 24:7). For me, in just three hours, God raised me up and delivered me.

Seven and three: completion and deliverance. My case didn't end in defeat, but in victory by God's grace.

I learned something unshakable that day: God's grace always manifests in the life of those who trust Him. His timing is perfect. His Word is true. And His sovereignty cannot be overturned.

To you who are reading this: whatever trial you're facing, whether in the courtroom, in your home, in your health, or in your soul, maintain your faith. What God said will manifest. Trust Him to do what He has promised, and you too will rise with a testimony that shouts louder than your trial.

THE VERDICT OF FREEDOM

That not guilty verdict did more than just free me from the weight of that case: it symbolized something far deeper, something eternal. The jury's declaration in that courtroom echoed a greater reality: there is now, therefore, no condemnation for those who are in Christ Jesus (Romans 8:1). That day, the gavel struck in my favor, but long before the jury ever filed back into that room, heaven had already declared me free. God had already spoken over my life: Not guilty! Not guilty of my past. Not guilty of my failures. Not guilty of the mistakes that once chained me.

When you surrender your life to Christ, He delivers you from the accusations of both the courtroom and the enemy's courtroom of condemnation. The devil is called the accuser of the brethren (Revelation 12:10), and he specializes in rehearsing your past in order to destroy your future. But the blood of Jesus silences every accusation. Just like the jury that day, heaven's verdict in Christ is clear: Case dismissed. Charges dropped. You are free.

Think about David, who should have been condemned for his failures as both king and man, but God still called him "a man after My own heart" (Acts 13:22). Think about Rahab, once a prostitute, but declared righteous by her faith and woven into the lineage of Jesus (Hebrews 11:31; Matthew 1:5). Think about Peter, who denied Jesus three times, but was restored and commissioned to "feed My sheep" (John 21:17). And Paul, once a persecutor of the church, later wrote two-thirds of the New Testament and boldly declared, "By the grace of God I am what I am" (1 Corinthians 15:10). Each of them bore the scars of their past, yet God stamped their lives with the verdict: Not guilty.

That's the power of surrender. Freedom doesn't come through fighting your own battles: it comes through submission to Jesus and allowing Him to take control of your life. It's about saying, "Lord, not my will but Yours be done" (Luke 22:42). And when you place your life in His hands, He takes the broken pieces, the painful chapters, and the guilty stains, and He rewrites your story with grace.

Yes, you may still have to walk through the consequences of your past decisions: David still lost his child, Moses still didn't enter the promised land, Paul still carried the memory of persecuting the church. But consequences are not condemnation. Because whom the Son sets free is free indeed (John 8:36).

On that day in court, I was liberated from a case, but the greater liberation had already happened when Christ saved me. That courtroom verdict was simply an earthly reflection of the heavenly verdict that was already written in the Lamb's Book of Life. God's grace declared me free long before man did.

So, to you reading this: hold your head high. Your past does not define you. Your mistakes do not sentence you. Your accuser does not have the final word. God does. And if you are in Christ Jesus, His word is eternal and unchanging: Not guilty.

God's declaration over your life, not guilty, is not just a moment; it's a movement. It is a daily walk of faith. You don't just stumble into freedom; you step into it through submission to Christ. Here are the key steps:

1. **REPENTANCE: TURNING FROM AND TURNING TO.** Repentance is more than feeling sorry: it is a change of direction. The Greek word metanoia means "to change one's mind." When Peter preached on Pentecost, his first command was simple yet life-changing: "Repent and be baptized, every one of you, in the name of Jesus Christ for the forgiveness of your sins" (Acts 2:38). Repentance is turning your back on sin and your face toward God. It is saying, "Lord, I don't just want to be forgiven—I want to be transformed."

2. **FAITH: TRUSTING GOD'S VERDICT OVER EVERY OTHER VOICE.** Faith is believing what God has said about you, even when your circumstances or your past scream otherwise. Abraham "believed God, and it was credited to him as righteousness" (Romans 4:3). Faith is choosing to trust that God's "not guilty" verdict is louder than the devil's accusations, the world's judgment, or your own doubts.

3. **OBEDIENCE: WALKING OUT WHAT GOD HAS DECLARED.** Obedience is the proof of submission. Jesus said, "If you love me, keep my commandments" (John 14:15). True freedom is not the liberty to do what you want: it's the power to do what God wills. When you obey Him, you live like a free man or woman because obedience keeps you in alignment with the One who has set you free.

4. **PRAYER: STAYING CONNECTED TO YOUR DEFENDER.** Prayer is your lifeline. Just as I sat in that courtroom with my attorney by my side, you have an Advocate with the Father: Jesus Christ, the righteous one (1 John 2:1). Through prayer, you stay connected to your Defender, who not only fights your battles but also whispers peace to your soul.

5. **WALKING IN THE SPIRIT: LIVING EMPOWERED, NOT CONDEMNED.** Paul writes, "Walk in the Spirit, and you will not gratify the desires of the flesh" (Galatians 5:16). The Holy Spirit empowers you to live beyond guilt and shame. He convicts, yes, but He never condemns. He strengthens you to walk in the freedom Christ purchased on the cross.

LIVING FREE, NOT CONDEMNED

You may still wrestle with the shadows of your past, but never forget that condemnation is a chain the enemy no longer has the key to. You are free. When you live in submission to Christ, His Spirit leads you, His Word guides you, and His grace covers you.

Submission is not bondage; it is the pathway to liberty. It is surrendering your will so you can experience God's will. And when you yield, the same God who stood with me in that courtroom will stand with you in every battle.

Remember this truth:

"Whom the Son sets free is free indeed" (John 8:36).

Not guilty of the charges. Not guilty of the shame. Not guilty of the past.

You are free and free indeed.

REFLECTION

1. When accusations rise against you, do you rest in the verdict of the courtroom or in the eternal verdict God has already spoken over your life?

2. What past mistakes are you still allowing the enemy to use to condemn you, even though God has already declared you not guilty?

3. Are you willing to surrender every area of your life to Christ so that His "not guilty" verdict becomes the foundation of your identity?

4. How does Romans 8:1, "There is therefore now no condemnation to those who are in Christ Jesus," reshape the way you see yourself?

5. When you hear the voice of condemnation in your mind, do you fight back with God's Word, or do you allow the accusations to define you?

6. What does submission to Christ look like in your daily life? Are there areas where you're resisting His authority?

7. Do you see faith as more than belief: as something to be lived out in forgiveness, obedience, and grace toward others?

8. Like Moses, Rahab, David, Peter, and Paul, can you identify the places where God has stamped not guilty over your own story?

9. When your faith is on trial, do your words and actions testify to your trust in God, or to your fear of people's opinions?

10. What steps of repentance, faith, obedience, prayer, and walking in the Spirit do you need to take to fully embrace your freedom in Christ?

11. Are you holding onto bitterness or unforgiveness when the freedom God gave you demands that you also extend forgiveness to others?

12. Do you truly believe that whom the Son sets free is free indeed, or are you still living as if you are bound by chains Christ already broke?

CHAPTER SIXTEEN

DREAMS
PART II

——◇◇◇——

THE BIG CASE WAS NOW IN THE REARVIEW mirror of my life. I was no longer staring into the darkness of uncertainty but humbly basking in the radiant light of God's deliverance. What the Lord had done for me was nothing short of breathtaking: a miracle of mercy, a testimony of His mighty hand. A weight that had long pressed against my chest was lifted, and for the first time in a long time, I could breathe freely. Yes, there was another case lingering, but compared to the one God had just brought me through, it seemed small. The shackles that once seemed permanent were beginning to loosen. I could sense it: freedom was not only near, but it was also tangible, visible, reachable.

In that moment of hope, my mind began to race toward the horizon of "what's next." I knew deep in my soul that God had called me to ministry. My spirit longed for training, for preparation, for equipping. I began to imagine myself in seminary halls, pouring over Scripture, sharpening my sword for the work of the Kingdom. I called my Aunt Theresa, the same aunt whom God had commissioned to visit me when I first got locked up, and I shared with her my desire to pursue theological education. With gentle conviction, she told me to look into a school called Moody Bible Institute. I had no information on it, but something in me knew to lock it in my heart. "When I get out," I thought, "I'll look into Moody."

That night, after lockup, I fell into a deep sleep. What happened next was unlike anything I had ever experienced. I had a dream: strange, vivid, and unforgettable.

In the dream, I stood in a magnificent gymnasium, the kind of place where professional basketball games are played. It was breathtaking in scale and beauty. As I walked out of the gym, I found myself in a maze-like hallway filled with classrooms. The corridors twisted and turned until I emerged by a food court bustling with life. Then the dream ended abruptly, but its weight pressed heavy on me when I woke the next morning.

As lockdown ended, I stepped into the dayroom and immediately noticed something unusual. Sitting at the table in the dayroom was a man I had never seen before. I knew chaplain Collen Bennette and Chaplain Roger Holmes, but this man I didn't know. He carried a small wooden case with a cross etched on it. I discovered that it was a case housing a small bible. I introduced myself and explained that I taught Bible studies in the pod. He smiled warmly and introduced himself: Pastor David Lester from Bloomington Bible Church, and, to my surprise, he stated that he was a graduate of Moody Bible Institute.

My heart skipped. "That's incredible," I said. "My aunt just told me about Moody as a place I should look into for ministry training."

I asked him to tell me more about the school. What he said next nearly knocked me out of my chair. He said, "They have the most beautiful gym you've ever seen, and some of the classrooms are underground in a maze-like formation."

At that very moment, I heard the Lord whisper in my spirit, "Think about what I showed you last night."

The presence of God radiated in me at that table like a holy flood. I shared my dream with Pastor Lester, and with tears in his eyes, he told me that God told him to come to the jail that day and when he arrives He will give him further instructions on what to do next. That encounter was the reason. He then gave me his card, offered to serve as a reference for my application to Moody, he prayed with me, and left.

I knew then and there that this was not a coincidence. This was divine orchestration. Pastor Lester had been sent on a prophetic assignment, an angel of sorts, to confirm what God had already revealed to me.

That encounter taught me something unforgettable: When God speaks, He also confirms. He leaves no stone unturned when it comes to mapping out your destiny. As

Jeremiah 29:11 declares, "For I know the plans I have for you, declares the LORD, plans to prosper you and not to harm you, plans to give you hope and a future."

Not long after, I had another dream: this one even clearer. I saw myself standing on top of a mountain, clothed in a robe, holding a shepherd's staff, and standing before a vast multitude of people. The message was undeniable: God had called me to be a shepherd to His people.

That Sunday, I went to the jail chapel service. The pastor stood to preach and admitted he had been wrestling with what message to bring. But when he arrived, the Spirit of God told him to preach a sermon entitled: "When You Dream Dreams." He preached about Joseph the dreamer in the book of Genesis, who, despite betrayal and prison, walked into his destiny. My soul leaped. It was God, again, confirming His word.

Fast forward to my release. When I walked into Moody Bible Institute, my dream unfolded in real time. The Solheim Center gymnasium was every bit as beautiful as I saw in the dream. The maze-like hallways of classrooms led me right into the dining area I had once wandered through in sleep.

I learned a very valuable lesson from that experience that says when you surrender your life to Christ, God Himself becomes the cartographer of your destiny. He maps out your path with precision, and He does not simply speak, He confirms. His word never returns void (Isaiah 55:11).

Think about Abraham. God promised him land, a lineage, and a legacy (Genesis 12). At first, all Abraham had was a word from God and a barren wife. Yet, every step of Abraham's journey, through altars, through famine, through trials, God confirmed His promise. When Abraham doubted, God took him outside and told him to look up at the stars. That was not astronomy, it was theological confirmation! What Abraham saw in the sky, God had already written in eternity.

Consider Joseph. God gave him a dream when he was just a teenager, showing him ruling over his brothers. That dream seemed impossible when he was betrayed, sold, falsely accused, and thrown into prison. But every prison cell was still a step on the divine map. At just the right time, God confirmed His word by elevating Joseph to Pharaoh's palace. The same brothers who mocked his dream bowed down before him, not because Joseph schemed it, but because God mapped it.

Look at Moses. Born under a death sentence, placed in a basket, raised in Pharaoh's palace, exiled to Midian, and then called from a burning bush. None of that was coincidence. God was ordering his steps and his stops. When Moses questioned his calling, God confirmed His promise with signs, wonders, and even the assurance, "I will be with you" (Exodus 3:12).

And then there's David. The prophet Samuel anointed him king while he was just a shepherd boy. That oil was the sign of the promise. But the throne did not come the next day. It took years of running from Saul, hiding in caves, and leading ragtag armies. Yet, every trial confirmed his calling. By the time he sat on the throne, David knew without a doubt that his life was mapped out by the hand of God.

The pattern is undeniable: promise, process, and confirmation. God speaks, God leads, God confirms. He did it for Abraham, Joseph, Moses, David, and He will do it for you.

This is why I need you to hear me with spiritual urgency: if you belong to Christ, your life is not a collection of random moments. It is a carefully orchestrated masterpiece. Every dream, every delay, every detour is part of the map. The same God who says, "I know the plans I have for you" (Jeremiah 29:11) is the God who also declares, "The steps of a good man (and woman) are ordered by the Lord" (Psalm 37:23).

And here's the persuasion: When you surrender your will to God, you don't have to figure out every turn because He already has. You don't have to force His hand because He will confirm His word. You don't have to fight for your future because God has already mapped it.

So, the question for you is this: will you trust the God who mapped out Abraham's steps, Joseph's dreams, Moses' mission, and David's destiny to also map out yours?

REFLECTION

1. Do you truly believe that God has mapped out your life, or do you struggle with trying to be your own architect?

2. How does knowing that "the steps of a good man are ordered by the Lord" (Psalm 37:23) affect the way you view your current season?

3. Can you recall a time when God confirmed something He had already promised you? How did that confirmation shape your faith?

4. In what ways has God spoken to you through dreams, Scripture, or people He strategically placed in your path?

5. What promises from God's Word are you currently holding onto, even if you haven't seen them fulfilled yet?

6. Are there areas in your life where you are resisting God's blueprint and trying to draw your own plans?

7. How do you discern between your own desires and God's divine direction for your life?

8. When you look back over your life, where do you see God's hand strategically aligning events, people, and places for your growth?

9. What fears or doubts keep you from trusting that God has already gone before you to prepare your future?

10. How do you respond when God's confirmation doesn't come immediately? Do you grow discouraged or deepen your trust?

11. What lessons can you draw from biblical figures like Joseph, Abraham, or Moses about waiting on God's mapped-out plan?

12. If you surrendered your future completely into God's hands today, what would that surrender look like in practical terms?

A SETBACK FOR A COMEBACK

THE TIME HAD FINALLY COME for me to face what I considered the "smaller case." Before a trial date was even set, I received a visit that pierced my soul. My children, along with their mother, came to see me. I was overjoyed to lay eyes on them, but my joy was fractured by the reality that I had to see them through a thick glass barrier. That glass was more than physical; it was emotional, spiritual, and deeply painful.

During that visit, the mother of my children looked me in the eye with frustration, sorrow, and longing. With a heavy voice, she told me, "We are ready for you to come home. The kids really miss you." Her words carried the weight of a thousand tears. I felt her pain. I felt my children's ache for their father. And in that moment, something in me shifted: I started thinking, scheming, and strategizing. My heart longed to speed the process up. Surely, there had to be a way to bypass a jury trial and find a shortcut home.

I rationalized it to myself. This was a probation case. I had no criminal history. I was a prime candidate for probation. I told myself, "I can handle probation. God has already changed my life, and I know I'm on a different path." After that visit, I met with my attorney, and he confirmed what I already believed, I was indeed a strong candidate for probation. My desire was simple... I just wanted to go home.

My attorney spoke with the Assistant Attorney General, and they presented another option, a "blind plea." In legal terms, it meant I would plead guilty without any agreement from the prosecution, leaving the sentencing solely in the hands of the judge. On paper, it seemed like a gamble, but in my heart, I thought it was an easy win. After all, what judge would send a man with no criminal record to prison when probation was on the table? This, I thought, was my way out.

To strengthen my case, my attorney lined up character witnesses. The courtroom was filled with people who knew me well: my mother, Doty (the man who once recruited me for his AAU basketball team and helped me secure a partial scholarship at Parkland College), and Reverend Colleen Bennette, the chaplain at McLean County Jail. Each one testified passionately on my behalf. My mother spoke with the tender authority of a loving mother. Doty recalled my leadership, my kindness, and the discipline I displayed on the court. Rev. Bennette testified about the man I had become behind bars, how I was teaching Bible study, leading men to Christ, and even preaching in Sunday services.

Letters poured in too. Letters that spoke of my transformation, my character, and my commitment to God. As each testimony rang out, my heart swelled with gratitude. It felt like a divine chorus affirming who I was becoming. My attorney gave a strong closing on my behalf. Everything seemed lined up perfectly. In my mind, the victory was sealed.

But then came the moment I will never forget. The judge cleared his throat, shuffled some papers, and began to speak. His words built up like storm clouds. Then came the thunder: "I sentence you to four years in the Illinois Department of Corrections."

The courtroom went silent. Those words were deafening, suffocating, crushing. My knees weakened. My spirit groaned. Tears flooded my eyes as disbelief washed over me. Four years? For a man with no criminal background? For a case where probation was clearly an option? My plan, the one I constructed so carefully, had failed.

When the judge allowed me to address the court, I stood there with trembling hands and a broken spirit. Through tears, I thanked him and declared what God had done in my life. I gave glory to the One who had rescued me even in my captivity. The judge listened and then spoke words that would echo in my soul: "If what you're doing now is true and genuine, the real test will be when you are released."

My family sat stunned, heartbroken, and shattered. As I blew them kisses, deputies led me away. Back in the pod, even fellow inmates were shocked. Everyone thought that day was my day to walk free. For days I sat in silence, numb from the blow. But then clarity came through the very newspaper that once ridiculed me. *The Pantagraph*, which had written disparaging articles when I was first jailed, now wrote a piece highlighting my testimony, my teaching, and my calling to ministry. They even reminded readers that I had been acquitted of the larger case and noted this smaller case had even less evidence.

And that's when the Spirit of God revealed the truth, I had made a critical mistake. In that dream I had that I spoke of in chapter 14, there were two wrestlers there, a big one and a small one. I went straight to the big one, and by faith, I overcame him. But I dismissed the small one, assuming victory was automatic. I never fought him in faith. In reality, that was the smaller case. My downfall was not the size of the opponent; it was the lack of faith in that moment. I let my longing for home outweigh my trust in God's timing.

The Bible says plainly, "Without faith it is impossible to please God" (Hebrews 11:6). My faith had been strong for the big case, but weak for the smaller one. Instead of relying on God's perfect plan, I leaned on my own understanding (Proverbs 3:5-6). And just like Adam and Eve in the garden, I allowed the serpent's whispers of doubt, shortcuts, and human reasoning, to lead me into disobedience. They forfeited Eden by trusting their own sight instead of God's Word. I forfeited freedom because I trusted my plan more than God's promise.

Yet even in that painful moment, God was not finished. What looked like a setback was simply a setup for a comeback. The same God who allowed Peter to fall into denial only to restore him with fire at Pentecost was the same God preparing my redemption.

Satan will always try to plant seeds of doubt, urging us to operate outside the will of God. But hear me: a faith that fizzles at the finish was flawed from the first. The enemy wants you to act prematurely so you miss the promise. But God wants you to trust patiently so you can walk in victory.

I learned a sobering truth: Delay does not mean denial. A prison sentence does not mean a canceled purpose. A setback is not the end; it is the soil for a greater comeback.

And so, with tears, I embraced the lesson. My plan failed, but God's plan never fails. My story was not over. This was only the beginning of a greater testimony.

Listen, never allow people, predicaments, or problems to pressure you into stepping outside the will of God. That is exactly where the enemy wants you: operating in panic rather than in promise, in fear rather than in faith, in self-will rather than in God's will. If God said it, then God will do it! You don't have to manipulate it, accelerate it, or fabricate it. Trust Him to work it out for your good.

I know the tension all too well. It often feels like heaven is moving in slow motion while your problems are rushing at full speed. It can appear as though God is taking a long time fulfilling His promise but hear me: delay does not mean denial. God's timetable is different from ours. What feels like a pause is often preparation. And what feels like punishment is often positioning.

Look at Zechariah (Luke 1:18-20). He doubted God's word when the angel declared that Elizabeth would bear a son. His disbelief resulted in a setback: he lost his voice and could not speak until John was born. His silence was a consequence of his skepticism. Yet, even in his setback, God's word still came to pass. John was born. The promise was fulfilled. And when Zechariah aligned his faith with God's truth, his tongue was loosed. His setback became the soil for a greater comeback.

Waiting is hard. I won't sugarcoat it. Waiting is a spiritual discipline that rubs against the grain of our human impulse. But it is far better to wait on God for a year than to rush ahead without Him for a day. The weight of waiting may be heavy, but the reward of waiting is holy.

So how do you wait well? How do you silence the whispers of the enemy who tells you, "God forgot about you... you better fix it yourself... He's not coming through"?

Here are five steps to waiting on God faithfully:

1. **ANCHOR YOURSELF IN GOD'S WORD** - When the enemy whispers lies, counteract with truth. Memorize and meditate on promises like Isaiah 40:31: "They that wait upon the LORD shall renew their strength." Let His Word be your weapon.

2. **SATURATE YOUR LIFE WITH PRAYER** - Prayer is not just asking, it's aligning. The more you commune with God, the less the enemy's chatter can penetrate your spirit.

3. **SURROUND YOURSELF WITH FAITH-FILLED VOICES** - Not everyone in your circle should have access to your spirit. Surround yourself with people who will remind you of God's promises when your faith feels fragile.

4. **SURRENDER THE TIMELINE** - Waiting requires relinquishing control. Say to God, "Not my will, but Yours be done, not my time but Yours." Remember: His timing is perfect even when it feels painful.

5. **STAND FIRM IN PRAISE** - Praise in the waiting is the ultimate declaration of trust. When you can worship in the hallway before the door opens, you're declaring that you trust the One who holds the key.

The devil thrives on impatience. He wants you to grab fruit before it ripens, to settle for Ishmael when God promised Isaac, to manufacture a blessing instead of manifesting in faith. But you must resist the urge to "help God out." When you wait on Him, you'll discover that what He's preparing for you is always worth the wait.

My setback taught me this: impatience will cost you more than patience ever will. But when you choose to wait, you position yourself for a comeback so great that it silences every whisper of doubt and magnifies the faithfulness of God.

REFLECTION

1. When you feel pressured by people or problems, do you find yourself moving in faith or reacting in fear?

2. What situations in your life tempt you to "help God out" rather than waiting on His timing?

3. How does Zechariah's story of doubt and delayed speech challenge you to trust God's promises even when they seem impossible?

4. Have you ever mistaken God's delay as His denial? What did you learn from that season?

5. In your current circumstances, do you believe God is preparing you, or do you believe He has forgotten you?

6. What scriptures can you anchor yourself in when the enemy whispers lies of discouragement?

7. Are you surrounding yourself with voices of faith or voices of fear in your waiting season?

8. What areas of your life do you need to surrender back to God's timeline today?

9. How would your perspective shift if you believed waiting is not wasted time but preparation time?

10. When was the last time you praised God before the promise was fulfilled? What did that do to your faith?

11. What would patience in this season cost you, and what would impatience cost you even more?

12. If you truly believed your setback is God's setup for a comeback, how would that change the way you live, wait, and worship right now?

CHAPTER EIGHTEEN
PRISON MINISTRY

THE DAY FINALLY CAME FOR ME to leave McLean County Jail and begin my journey into the Illinois Department of Corrections. My time of county confinement was over, and now I would be transferred into the very system I once thought I would never see from the inside. Before I left, I passed the baton of leadership to my brother Josh: a man who had once been a devout Muslim but, by the grace of God, converted to Christianity and had become one of the most faithful attendees in our Bible study. That moment was bittersweet. Hugs, handshakes, and words of encouragement filled the air, but then the shackles were placed on my wrists and ankles, chaining me to others who, like me, were waiting for judgment to run its course.

We boarded the bus, shackled side by side, and watched the free world roll by outside the window: families driving home, children playing, life happening. It felt as if we were ghosts moving past a life we no longer belonged to. The bus arrived at Joliet Prison, the massive gates groaning open only to slam shut with a deafening clang behind us. That sound wasn't just metal hitting metal. It was the echo of lost freedom, a sound that could crush your spirit if you let it.

Joliet was not to be my final stop, only a holding station until my permanent assignment arrived in the form of a brown paper bag. For one week, I remained there, on near-constant lockdown, awakened each morning by officers banging steel rods against iron bars in harsh rhythm. That sound jarred me awake every day like a reminder that mercy doesn't come from man but from God alone. Finally, the day came. My brown bag revealed my destination: Logan Correctional Facility, a medium-security prison in downstate Illinois.

When I arrived at Logan, I was assigned to a unit. Just like at Cook County Jail, the first question was asked, "What gang are you with?" And once again, I rejoiced in the power of being able to say with confidence: "None."

Freedom is not just the absence of chains; it is the power to not be defined by the labels others want to place on you.

Ironically, I was recognized by a few men, one of them a former teammate from Parkland College who embraced me warmly. I was given a prison job, a wage so small it could only be described as modern-day slavery, but it put something on my books and gave me a small sense of contribution.

Then came a pivotal moment in my story. I heard about a drug program called Gateway, a drug rehabilitation initiative. If accepted, the program could reduce my sentence. On the application, there was a question: "Were you a drug user?" I checked yes, even though it was a lie. My crime was selling, not using. That small lie filled me with conviction.

The day came when the program representative called my name. With the weight of the Holy Spirit pressing on my heart, I confessed, "Sir, I lied on the application. I wasn't a user; I was a drug dealer. I'm sorry I wasn't truthful."

He looked at me and, with words I'll never forget, said, "This program is for you too. Just as the addict was addicted to using, you were addicted to selling for your own gain. You belong here because your addiction was just as destructive, maybe even more so."

In that moment, the grace of God met me in an unlikely place. My honesty became the key to my acceptance. And more than that, it became a lesson that integrity will take you further than deception ever could.

Soon after, I was transferred into the Gateway unit, housed away from general population. We lived in four-man rooms, not cells, and our days were filled with group meetings that often turned into rivers of tears. Trauma, pain, and brokenness poured out of men who had known nothing but chaos. In that broken place, God gave me an assignment. I started a Bible study. Night after night, it grew. Men gave their lives to Christ. Souls were saved in the very place meant to cage us.

I'll never forget one Sunday service. A ministry team from the outside came in with a small pool set up for baptism. Twenty-five men from our unit stood up to be baptized. But when asked, "Do you want to receive Jesus Christ as your Lord and Savior?" they all replied, "We already have."

Confused, the preacher asked, "Well, who led you to Christ?"

And with one accord, they pointed in my direction and said: "That man right there. He teaches us the Word every night."

At that moment, tears filled my eyes. It wasn't pride; it was purpose. Behind prison bars, surrounded by steel and concrete, God had turned captivity into a pulpit. What the devil meant for evil, God was using for good (Genesis 50:20).

That day, all twenty-five men were baptized. And that day, I realized something I will carry for the rest of my life: Prison cannot chain the Gospel. Circumstances cannot cancel your calling. Bars cannot block the move of God. Chains don't choke callings; shackles don't silence the Spirit. Prison may have walls, but it cannot wall off the Word of God.

I made up my mind in the middle of confinement: I refuse to let prison incarcerate my mind. The walls could hold my body, but they could not hold my faith. The locks could restrain my movements, but they could not restrain my mission. The guards could watch over my days, but they could not watch over the fire burning in my soul. I knew that the only way to get through it was to change how I viewed it. Yes, it was a place of confinement, but I chose to see it as a place of consecration. Yes, it was a place of restriction, but I chose to see it as a place of release: where my ministry could break forth in ways I never imagined.

I stopped seeing prison as the end of my story, and I started seeing it as a chapter in God's greater narrative. Like Joseph in Pharaoh's dungeon, like Jeremiah in the cistern, like Paul in Rome, I realized that confinement is not cancellation. It is simply the classroom where God trains His servants.

So, I shifted my perspective. Those men around me were not just fellow inmates, they were souls. Souls loved by

God. Souls bound not just by chains of steel but by chains of sin, despair, addiction, and hopelessness. And I knew the gospel was not just something to be preached from pulpits in polished sanctuaries, it had to be lived out in chains.

When God showed me my purpose, I made the decision that I would live it out before my outdate. I would not wait until the doors opened to start ministry; I would start ministry right there, in the middle of my confinement. Yes, there were activities I enjoyed: basketball on the yard, working out in the rec, passing time in ordinary ways, but none of those compared to the fire that came alive when I served God in chains. That was the real work. That was the eternal work.

And here's the revelation, when you give yourself to the work of God, even in prison, time is no longer slow and stagnant. It becomes meaningful. It becomes substantive. Every conversation, every prayer, every Bible study, every testimony turned into holy ground. What should have felt like wasted days became sacred days. What should have been lost time became redeemed time.

I witnessed lives changed, hearts transformed, destinies altered. I watched men who had given up on themselves find hope in Christ. I saw those who thought they were forgotten discovering they were remembered by God. I saw men who walked into that prison one way walk out forever changed. And I came to know in the deepest parts of my soul that God doesn't just send you through a prison; sometimes He plants you in a prison so that others can be set free.

Your "prison" may not have concrete walls or iron bars: it may be the prison of grief, the prison of debt, the prison of illness, or the prison of regret, but the principle remains: if you can change how you view it, God can change how you live in it. Stop counting the days and start making the days count. Stop waiting for freedom to serve and start serving where you are. Don't sit in silence when God is calling you to sing in the midnight. Don't waste your waiting, work your waiting.

Because here is the truth: when you serve God in chains, you discover that chains don't diminish destiny, they define it. Chains don't silence your witness, they amplify it.

Chains don't slow you down, they position you for impact. And when God is ready, He will not just bring you out, He will bring you out stronger, wiser, bolder, and more anointed than you were when you went in.

And I can hear somebody saying right now, "But I feel lost... I feel like time is slipping away from me... I feel like I've wasted too many years." Let me tell you this with the full weight of God's truth: you still have purpose.

The passing of time does not cancel the plan of God. Just because the clock is ticking does not mean your calling is over. There are gifts that God has placed on the inside of you: divine deposits that were planted in your spirit before you ever took your first breath. Those gifts are not dormant; they are waiting. Waiting for you to stir them. Waiting for you to trust them. Waiting for you to release them into a world that is starving for what only you carry. And hear me: those gifts are not just for you, but they are also designed to change the lives of every person you come in contact with. So, stop seeing your current place as only a place of pain. See it as a place of purpose. Stop labeling it as a prison of despair. Redefine it as a platform for destiny. Don't look at your circumstances as punishment; see them as preparation. God has a way of transforming the very ground that feels barren into fertile soil. He has a way of bringing forth fruit in the most unlikely places.

REFLECTION

1. Where in your life do you feel "stuck," and could it be that God is calling you to see that place as purposeful rather than painful?

2. What gifts or talents has God placed inside of you that you've been neglecting or hiding?

3. How can you start using your gifts right now, even in small ways, to impact those around you?

4. Do you see your current season as punishment, or are you willing to see it as God's preparation?

5. How has God already brought beauty out of brokenness in your past, and what does that reveal about His power to do it again in your life?

6. When you hear the phrase "God can grow roses out of concrete," what does that mean for you personally?

7. Have you allowed pain, disappointment, or confinement to incarcerate your mind instead of liberating your purpose?

8. How are you using your time right now? Are you using it wisely, or are you letting it slip away?

9. Are you spending more time focusing on what you've lost, or are you focusing on what you can gain through God's purpose for you?

10. What would it look like for you to consecrate your current place rather than curse it?

11. Could your personal struggles become a testimony that transforms someone else's life if you faithfully live out your purpose right where you are?

12. Are you willing to trust that God's timing, even if it feels delayed, is still perfect for your destiny?

CHAPTER NINETEEN

LIBERATED BY GRACE

I CANNOT TELL YOU the exact date marked on the calendar of my release, but I can tell you the month was June of 1996. That June was a month of destiny. As the days crawled toward my freedom, time felt like it was working against me. That final week behind bars stretched on like an endless night. Every tick of the clock was a tug on my soul, every sunset a reminder that I was still behind the walls when my heart was already running ahead toward my family.

I dreamed of wrapping my arms around my children, of sitting at the table with my mother and grandmother, of worshiping in church without the echoes of chains clinking in the background. I dreamed of laughter replacing lament. I dreamed of purpose replacing pain.

I had finished the program, my time was cut, and when the day of release arrived, my emotions were colliding. I had joy on one side and fear on the other. I was afraid that they were going to come and tell me that they'd found another reason to keep me locked down. That was nothing but the enemy trying to play tricks with my mind. I also had a small sense of sadness because in the Gateway Unit, we had become more than inmates, we were a family, bound not by blood but by brokenness, stitched together by survival and hope. I felt an attachment to them, but the joy of my freedom outweighed all of that.

When the gates of Logan Correctional Center finally opened, I was given a $100 check, a change of clothes that my family had faithfully brought for me, and a Greyhound bus ticket. That was the currency of my new beginning. Think about it, years of my life traded for a hundred dollars, a new outfit, and a seat on a bus. But what they gave me in my hands could not compare to what God had already deposited in my heart.

I stepped outside those gates, and the world looked different. The air was fresher. The sun seemed brighter. Even the dirt beneath my shoes felt sacred. I was free. My mind raced with plans that included a McDonald's hamburger, playing with my children, embracing my children, hugging my mother, sitting at my grandmother's table, worshiping in church, walking into Moody Bible Institute to start a new chapter in education and ministry. My list was long, but my joy was longer.

Then, while sitting on that Greyhound bus heading home, something hit me like a revelation from heaven. That bus was not the first. My journey had been marked by five buses:

- The first bus carried me to Cook County Jail.

- The second bus took me to McLean County Jail.

- The third bus transported me to Joliet State Prison.

- The fourth bus delivered me to Logan Correctional Center.

- And now this fifth bus... this one was different. This one was not taking me deeper into captivity, it was ushering me into freedom.

Five buses. Five chapters of my captivity. And then God spoke through the numbers. In Scripture, the number five is the number of God's grace. His grace was written into my journey, woven into the fabric of my story. His grace carried me through the darkness of confinement and now was carrying me into the dawn of deliverance.

At that moment, I realized I was not just a man leaving prison, I was a man liberated by God's grace. Another word for grace is favor. And favor means that God tilted the scales in my direction, not because of my merit, but because of His mercy. I was favored to live when I could have died. Favored to be free when I could have still been bound. Favored to step into destiny when the enemy wanted me destroyed.

Let me tell you this: there is a beauty in freedom that chains can never comprehend. To be free is not just to walk outside of prison walls; it is to walk into divine purpose. Freedom is not just about what you leave behind, it's about what you are called to step into. I no longer had to sit on buses staring out barred windows while life passed me by. No, this time, I was free to live the life God had consecrated me for.

I was free to hug my children. Free to honor my mother and grandmother. Free to eat what I wanted. Free to go where I wanted. Free to make free phone calls. Free to raise my hands in worship in a church sanctuary without shackles. Free to enroll in Moody Bible Institute and prepare for the ministry God had ordained for me before the foundations of the world.

Grace had met me in Cook County. Grace had sustained me in Joliet. Grace had preserved me in Logan. And grace rode with me on that fifth bus all the way home.

I did not just walk out of prison; I walked into promise. I did not just leave behind a sentence; I stepped into a Savior's embrace. I was not simply released by the system; I was liberated by the Spirit.

June of 1996 was not just a date of release. It was a declaration of destiny. That day showed that God's grace doesn't just save, it sets free. And that day, I could say with all conviction: God met me there and His grace never left me, and I never looked back when God.

In the spring of 2000, I enrolled at Moody Bible Institute. The very place I had once seen only in dreams became the soil of my reality. And in 2004, by the grace of God, I walked across that stage and graduated with a Bachelor of Science Degree in Pastoral/Integrated Ministry Studies. That degree was not just a piece of paper; it was a testimony. It declared to the world that God can take a prisoner and turn him into a preacher. He can take a felon and turn him into a father, a husband, a shepherd of souls, a servant of His kingdom.

For over twenty years now, I have had the privilege of pastoring the New Israelite Missionary Baptist Church on the South Side of Chicago. What once was a broken voice has become a prophetic voice in the pulpit, calling men and women to the same freedom I found in Christ.

My children are thriving, living testimonies of God's restoring power. And God, in His infinite wisdom, blessed me with my soul mate, Rayna Andrews, the love of my life, the partner of my purpose, the one who has walked with me in joy and in journey, in faith and in fulfillment.

But God's story in me did not stop there. In the spring of 2026, I will graduate from North Park Theological Seminary with a Master's Degree in Christian Formation, and then press onward in pursuit of a PhD in Public Theology and Community Engagement. Each step of the way, God has been writing chapters of grace into my life: chapters that no prison wall could contain, no record could erase, no enemy could cancel.

And here is the truth I want you to carry from these pages: my story is not an isolated one. It is not unique to me alone. The same God who met me at my lowest point, the same God who found me in chains and navigated me toward freedom, is the same God who can meet you right where you are.

Maybe your prison is not made of bars and razor wire. Maybe your prison is addiction. Maybe it's depression. Maybe it's fear, shame, bitterness, or regret. Whatever your prison may be, hear me clearly: God can meet you there. He is not intimidated by the walls that surround you, nor is He bound by the failures that define you. He is the God who steps into broken places and brings beauty, who takes concrete and grows roses, who takes the ashes of a life and breathes into them a testimony of freedom.

All you must do is trust Him. Trust Him as your personal Lord and Savior. Trust Him enough to hand Him the pen and let Him rewrite the story of your life. Trust Him enough to let Him redefine your pain into purpose, and your captivity into calling.

I stand as living proof that God still liberates, God still transforms, God still redeems, and God still restores. And I declare to you with every fiber of my being: He will meet you too.

Wherever you are. However, broken you feel. However long you've been waiting. He will meet you. Because that's who

He is: the God who comes near, the God who steps in, the God who delivers, the God who sets free.

This is my story, but it can be yours as well.

God met me there and He can meet you there.

God bless you!

MY PRAYER FOR YOU

*Father, I thank You that You are the God who meets us where
we are. You met me in my prison, and You brought me into freedom. Now
I ask that You meet the one who is holding this book.*

*Lord, step into their valley, into their struggle, into their
brokenness. Remind them that they are not forgotten, not forsaken, not
beyond Your reach.
Let them feel the weight of chains falling off even now.*

*Jesus, I declare freedom over their life: freedom from sin, freedom
from shame, freedom from every prison of the soul. Fill them with new
vision, new purpose, new hope.*

*Holy Spirit, breathe fresh fire into their heart. Let them know
beyond a shadow of a doubt that You have called them, that You love
them, that You have destined them for more.*

*God, may their story become a testimony of Your grace.
May they walk into new doors, new opportunities, and new levels of
freedom.
And may they one day be able to declare, with boldness and joy:
"God met me here... and He set me free."*

In the mighty, matchless, marvelous name of Jesus I pray, Amen.

ABOUT THE AUTHOR

CHENIER ALSTON is a biblical scholar, teacher, visionary leader, pastor, and passionate advocate for social justice whose life is rooted in faith, service, and transformation. For over 20 years, he has faithfully served as Senior Pastor of New Israelite Missionary Baptist Church in Chicago, guiding souls toward Christ and championing hope in his community.

A native of Chicago Heights, Illinois, Chenier's life was forever changed in the summer of 1995 when he encountered God in what he calls his "burning bush experience." That moment ignited his calling and set him on a journey from brokenness to freedom—one marked by grace, resilience, and unwavering purpose.

A graduate of Moody Bible Institute, Chenier holds a Bachelor of Science in Integrated Ministry Studies and is currently pursuing a Master's in Christian Formation at North Park University, with plans for a PhD in Public Theology and Community Engagement.

Beyond the pulpit, Chenier is a devoted husband to Rayna, a proud father and grandfather, an author, teacher, and servant-leader whose ministry continues to inspire lives with one timeless truth: God still meets us in the low places and leads us into freedom.

www.ingramcontent.com/pod-product-compliance
Lightning Source LLC
Chambersburg PA
CBHW060053100426
42742CB00014B/2802